PICKING RIGHT

THE SINGLE'S GUIDE TO
FINDING THE RIGHT MATCH

PICKING RIGHT

THE SINGLE'S GUIDE TO FINDING THE RIGHT MATCH

DAPHNA LEVY

Golden MILLENNIUM productions PUBLISHING

PICKING RIGHT
The Single's Guide to Finding the Right Match
by Daphna Levy

www.PickingRight.com
www.TheSecretsOfHappilyEverAfter.com

Published by Golden Millennium Productions, Inc.
www.GoldenProductions.com

©2014, 2017 by Daphna Levy-Hernandez

Paperback ISBN: 978-1-886668-98-0
Paperback first edition 2017
Printed in the United States of America

Library of Congress Cataloging-in-Publication Data

Daphna Levy
PICKING RIGHT
The Single's Guide to Finding the Right Match

Paperback ISBN: 978-1-886668-98-0
Library of Congress Control Number: 2016960474
Paperback first edition 2017

Contents

Acknowledgments

To my husband, who has been "the wind beneath my wings," my cheerleader, brainstorming partner and best friend; who tirelessly pushed and inspired me to share my passion and expertise in helping others, and my insight as "the best wife."

Life is a team effort, really. And so I thank my dedicated team, my friends, my mentors and my clients. I couldn't have done it without you.

Thank you to my friend and renowned Syrian author Gladys Matar for sharing her hard-won wisdom with me.

To Leona Fine for helping unleash my writing ability.

To L. Ron Hubbard for teaching me how to help and for providing the inspiration for the exercises in this book.

To Starr O'Malley Engelhart for her steady and reliable guidance.

To fine-art and portrait artist Christine Sargent for being my loyal "artist friend."

To Pearl Lantz, Sigal Adini and Pat Lusey for their help and support.

To Rosemary Delderfield for editing and proofreading.

To Eugenia May-Montt for art direction, cover and book design.

And to Lea Frechette for typography and graphic production.

The list goes on. But you know who you are, and you have my love and gratitude.

TESTIMONIAL
From Picking Wrong to the Altar and Beyond

Dear Daphna,

I read your book, Picking Right, *around July 2014. I love it! The information in it was vital for me because I would always choose wrong. Your book made so much sense and gave me clarity on my love life.*

At the time I was in a wrong relationship, on and off. I knew it was wrong. The book just confirmed it. But it also gave me hope because I always believed that my true partner was out there somewhere! Somebody whom I love, respect and admire and who respects me, loves and admires me, and where we can support each other and grow together.

Your book made it easier for me to see what I wanted and what I was looking for and be certain about it. It's a must-read book for anyone so they don't get trapped in the wrong relationships.

Anyway, I met Zoltan, my husband, in November 2014. We started dating in March 2015 and we got married in May. He is a great man and a great husband. My family loves him and he loves them back. In fact, our love has brought my family together. Our marriage is beautiful! We do have our life challenges, but we support each other and so get through them.

Daphna, your book put me in control of my life. Thank you so much!!!

Pamela Dicso-Caceres

WHO THIS BOOK IS FOR

 This book is not a pick-up guide or an attraction manual. It was not written to teach women how to get men drooling over them; nor was it meant to teach men how to be popular with the ladies. It is not about the right thing to say on the first date, or how long you should wait before calling him/her back. And it certainly is not about changing who you really are in an effort to attract the opposite sex!

Perhaps there *are* rules for the game of dating. They may be valid and workable if you are out to have what some call a "good time." That is not what this book is about.

If you've "been there, done that," have been around the block a few times and are ready for a meaningful, long-lasting relationship, then different rules must apply. Or if you are *new* to the dating game, why not learn how to Pick Right straightaway and avoid the drama and heartbreaks you see all around you?

After all, how can you identify a compatible mate if you spend the first few weeks or months of dating faking it, acting, not being yourself? And how will *you* recognize *your* perfect match, if he or she is doing the same thing?

You need tools to help you Pick Right and make the relationship grow or to recognize when it's wrong and move on. You want to be able to predict future trouble *before* it occurs. You want to identify poor compatibility before you waste any more time. Recognize the cheater before they cheat. Identify the gold digger before they dig. And know the person who can't return your affection before you give your heart away.

You don't want to look back after the fact and say, "I should have known better!" In short, you want to invest yourself in a relationship that truly has the potential of being your dream come true.

This book is for people who wish to create a lifelong fulfilling relationship—a relationship that elevates both of you, makes each of you better and stronger, and empowers you to achieve your personal goals, to help one another and even to help the world.

Does this sound unreal? Too good to be true? Perhaps. But read on. What do you have to lose?

WARNING/DISCLAIMER

Use the advice in this book at your own risk. The author and the publisher take no responsibility for any breakups resulting from you opening your eyes, nor will they be responsible for any happy, long-lasting relationships developing from your newfound insight.

Furthermore, don't blame them if you create that rare family where children are raised by their biological parents and love persists into your golden years and beyond.

Additionally, the happy noise in your home is not their fault. Happy, healthy children can be noisy. You'll get used to it!

This book is meant to both educate and entertain. The intention is to provide accurate and helpful information on the subject matter. You may find more wisdom about it here than anywhere else, and may also discover that it echoes what you have always believed to be true but found no one who would agree with you.

Picking Right is not a relationship quick fix. Relationships take hard, honest work as well as true understanding of the mind and life. Many people who are happy in their relationships, however, do live by the guidelines covered herein.

The responsibility for the use of this information is yours, and neither the author nor the publisher takes any responsibility for the consequences. You read this book with the understanding that the author and publisher are not rendering relationship counseling through its text. If you are in need of relationship help, you may seek advice from a competent professional. Every effort has been made to present the various principles as clearly as possible. The author and publisher cannot take responsibility for any misinterpretations by the reader. They have neither liability nor responsibility to any person or entity with respect to any damage or loss caused, or alleged to be caused, directly or indirectly by the information contained in this book. They have no responsibility for omissions or inaccuracies, nor liability for risk or loss of anything related to anyone's personal or financial well-being that may have been incurred directly or indirectly from any advice given or implied herein.

If you do not wish to be bound by the above, you may return this book to the publisher for a full refund.

INTRODUCTION

If you have ever had a failed relationship—and who hasn't?—perhaps you looked back after the fact and said, "What was I thinking? We were *not* right for each other from the start!" You at last saw with clarity that the relationship had been doomed to fail. Yet such enlightenment escaped you at the outset.

We get attracted to the opposite sex for the strangest reasons: from her manicured nails to the size of his biceps; from the sex appeal of body parts to the "real-man" look of a tool belt; from admiration to pity; from need to desire.

> *"We are all a little weird and*
> *Life's a little weird,*
> *And when we find someone whose*
> *Weirdness is compatible with ours,*
> *We join up with them and fall in*
> *Mutual weirdness and call it Love."*
> —Dr. Seuss

Two people who are attracted to each other might stick together in misery for life. So *attraction* doesn't guarantee that you are a match.

There is comparable education and social status, similar upbringing and cultural background. We hope to find in those a sound foundation for a happy relationship. Yet we know people who were a match in that respect and still failed.

Then there is compatibility in terms of goals and careers: both people are lawyers, physicians, blue-collar workers or the executive type; both are artists or entertainers. However, relationship failure can be found in all walks of life. Therefore professional compatibility provides no guarantee.

How about being different from each other? Some people say "opposites attract." So you find your opposite and rely on your differences to provide excitement and positive challenge. But we've witnessed failure there as well.

A RAY OF HOPE

Is there a right way to choose a mate, or is it just a matter of luck? Can anything be done to avoid the failure that is the fate of so many relationships?

Let's define *failure*. Failure isn't just a divorce or a breakup. An unhappy relationship, with partners putting up with each other for the kids' sake or out of fear of change, is as much of a failure as any breakup. Such a relationship is void of love, warmth, friendship and joy—the elements that make relationships worthwhile.

Looking around at unhappy or ruined relationships, you may have concluded that being happy in a relationship is but a childish dream. After all, most people live a compromise. Few seem happy and fulfilled in their relationships. Perhaps you've even told yourself to "grow up," become "realistic" and stop reaching for the stars. Certainly, others have urged you to compromise your goals and dreams. That's because people who have given up on their own dreams tend to recruit others for the Failure Brigade—it alleviates their loneliness.

However, since you are reading this book, I trust you still have a ray of hope. I *hope* you do, because on the day that you give up a dream, you die a little. People don't die all at once. They die in stages: one dream at a time. Possibly, an individual could practically rise from the dead if his or her hopes were restored.

The reason I chose to share the following story with you is not because it has to do with relationships (it doesn't), but because it illustrates the vital role that goals play in life, and how detrimental losing them can be.

Many years ago my husband had an employee he was very fond of. Sal had worked for a supply house until he retired. He was in his seventies when Robert ran into him again and he looked pale, sick and ready to kick the bucket. Retirement was killing him: he had no goals and very little to live for. Robert had never forgotten how Sal had helped him in his early days in business, giving him tips and teaching the ropes to an ambitious young man. It was time to return the favor, so he asked Sal to come and work for him.

Sal got a new lease on life. Work gave him new goals. His health miraculously improved, and he went on to be productive on the job for nearly a decade. It wasn't until his wife died that he once again lost the will to live. He passed away shortly afterwards.

That is the power of goals and dreams. So don't give up on yours!

> *"If you want to live a happy life,*
> *tie it to a goal,*
> *not to people or things."*
> —Albert Einstein

PICKING WRONG

Perhaps we want to find our match and build a happy, long-lasting relationship. However, if the selection process is faulty, a relationship is doomed to fail. Picking Right permits stability, harmony and happiness. Picking Wrong creates challenges and potential trouble. Unfortunately, many people repeat their mistakes: having found trouble with a certain personality type, they often pick the same type in the next relationship. As one woman said while comparing her boyfriend to her ex-husband, "Maybe I saw my husband in him."

Why do people Pick Wrong? How come they fail to learn from experience? Why do they persist on this path of self-destruction? When cupid strikes, they seem to lose control of their emotions or willpower, like a hypnotized subject who can't control how he feels about smoking cigarettes or eating pie. Consequently, they can't make correct decisions that would elevate and improve their life.

This book seeks to equip and empower you to Pick Right so that you may attain the happiness you are in search of. It is based on a profound understanding of human nature and on years of experience helping individuals and couples with their lives and relationships. Whether a successful businessman, a famous artist or a "regular" person (although we are all special in our own unique way), the state of our relationships impacts each and every one of us.

Relationships can make or break us. They can make the wealthy sad and the successful depressed. On the other hand, a good relationship can make even the poor rich in a way that money cannot.

WHAT ARE THE GUARANTEES?

Life offers no guarantees in any department, and relationships are no exception. Even two people who are a perfect match face challenges in maintaining their relationship and keeping it young and fresh. Even they could spoil their best chances by doing all the wrong things.

Fortunately, there *are* principles and guidelines to a successful relationship. They are not taught in school or in most families. If you know and use them, you could—by your own actions as a couple—guarantee the success of your union.

Although this book is about Picking Right, it contains some of the secrets to *building* and *maintaining* a happy relationship. But primarily it provides the knowledge and tools you need to Pick Right, so that the two of you may *have* a fighting chance.

> *"Knowledge is power only*
> *if man knows what facts*
> *not to bother with."*
> —Robert Staughton Lynd

CHAPTER 1

RELATIONSHIPS: BACK TO BASICS

CHAPTER 1

RELATIONSHIPS: BACK TO BASICS

Any truly committed relationship—including a marriage—is a partnership, a union, a bond. And the greater the commitment, the more of a partnership it is.

But what is the *purpose* of a relationship? What is "love"? Is there a route that leads to happiness? How well do we understand these subjects? Yet regardless of whether or not we do, we get involved in relationships, and our lives get deeply impacted by their short- and long-term consequences.

THE CONFUSIONS OF OUR LOVE LIFE

In navigating the world of computers, cars, law, investments, medicine, real estate, engineering, flying planes—you name it—we recognize the necessity to understand each subject. We hire a professional, such as an attorney or an accountant, because they understand law or taxes. We go to doctors because they understand the workings of the body. But do we understand love, relationships, marriage?

Certainly, we've been told a great deal about them. We may have read books and watched romantic movies; but judging by the trouble we find ourselves in, could it be that we don't know all there is to know about these subjects? Could it be that, unlike breathing or learning to walk, relationship wisdom is not intuitive?

It is safe to say that society as a whole is in a state of confusion with regard to relationships. If you consult your parents, friends or neighborhood therapist, you will get a wide variety of views and opinions—some of them conflicting. Each person you talk to draws from their own experience, failures and pain. There seems to be no truth, nothing to sink your teeth into and say, "This is the way things really are!"

Adding to the confusion is the fact that two people starting a relationship are not always embarking upon the same activity, because *relationship* means one thing to one of them and something else entirely to the other. Such divergent visions are a recipe for disaster.

What would happen if you truly understood relationships? Wouldn't such understanding help and improve your life?

A computer expert can handle computers successfully because he understands them. A good mechanic knows cars and so keeps them running. An engineer who knows bridge building constructs bridges that can be crossed safely and that withstand natural disasters.

Evidently, true understanding is the key to success.

If we understood relationships, we could better survive the storms of life. We could create a relationship and keep it going like a well-maintained car that takes us safely on our journey. And most probably, we would also enjoy the ride!

> *"An investment in knowledge*
> *always pays the best interest."*
> —Benjamin Franklin

WHAT ARE RELATIONSHIPS FOR?

A relationship is a union between two individuals, and the best way to understand it is to understand its purpose. What is it for?

Why do we go through all that trouble?

A relationship is supposed *to assist and improve the life, health, happiness and success of the partners in that relationship* (including any little ones who may join them later on).

Many relationships have the opposite effect: instead of improving both people's lives, they worsen them. Such a relationship would be as beneficial as owning a car you must carry on your back.

If the purpose of a relationship is to *improve* life, let's stop settling for relationships that deteriorate it, and let's work to elevate our relationships to a level that contributes to a better existence for all concerned.

> *"Nothing in life is as good*
> *as the marriage of true minds*
> *between man and woman.*
> *As good? It is life itself."*
> —Pearl Buck

THE MATH OF RELATIONSHIPS

When it comes to relationships there is an equation: $1 + 1$ should $=$ *at least* 2.

Two people might reflect on their lives before they met and compare them to their current state. Taking into account personal goals and dreams, happiness, career, productivity, even health— whatever is important to them—has their union contributed to their individual success and well-being, or has it detracted from it?

$1 + 1 = 2$ means that each of them is doing as well in the relationship as they did before they met. In other words, the relationship has not worsened their lives (but hasn't enhanced them either).

11

That is not as bad as Picking Wrong. When you Pick Wrong, the sum of two individuals is less than two. Together, they are being and doing less than they did individually. The relationship *drains* rather than *empowers* them. It makes them grow smaller and achieve less. If they cannot remedy the situation despite honest efforts, it may be time to face the fact that they have Picked Wrong.

The following real-life story is an example of a union that had a negative effect on its members.

When Bob and Sally met, Sally had been pursuing a career, something Bob admired about her. However, as soon as they got married, life became all about "us." She had no more personal goals, and she constantly required his attention. This was a drain on Bob and even had a bad effect on his career. "Us" resulted in a weaker and unhappier he and she.

Conversely, when the Pick is truly Right, 1 + 1 = 3 or 4 or more. Both people thrive in the relationship. They are happier and more fulfilled than before. They accomplish more, both individually and as a team. They become more successful. They reach out and make their dreams come true. Perhaps they even accomplish things they never before thought possible because now, with a genuine friend and cheerleader by their side, they are truly empowered.

Barbara and Gary were one such a couple.

When they met, Gary owned a young construction company, while Barbara worked a low-level office job. Gary encouraged her to take a better job and later on helped her start her own business.

Early in the relationship, Barbara learned that visitation issues prevented Gary from seeing his son from a previous relationship. She took it upon herself to address the matter and succeeded in reuniting the son with his father.

As a team, Gary and Barbara established a nonprofit to help their community. They lived in harmony and were always there for each other. And they accomplished more together than they had individually. One might say that, thanks to their relationship, they each lived a "bigger life."

Such relationships may be rare, but they do exist. While this is the *ideal* for a relationship, it *is* attainable. Nothing is more inspiring than seeing couples living the *relationship equation* correctly. And it all starts with Picking Right.

> **"It is the man and woman united**
> **that make the complete**
> **human being."**
> —Benjamin Franklin

EXERCISE 1
The Math of Relationships

You have undoubtedly witnessed or been in relationships that impacted the partners in varying degrees: some improved the partners' lives, some worsened them, while others made little difference. Let's look at some of these relationships and practice the *Math of Relationships*.

Think of a relationship, yours or someone else's, where

a) $1 + 1 = 2$

The relationship did not change the partners' individual lives: they were not better off together than they had been before the relationship, but they were not worse off either.

* * *

b) $1 + 1 =$ less than 2

The relationship worsened the partners' individual lives: they were worse off together than they were before the relationship.

* * *

c) $1 + 1 =$ more than 2

The relationship enhanced the partners' individual lives and they were much better off together than before the relationship.

* * *

Go through a, b, c and then again a, b, c until you can easily estimate the value of any relationship using the *Math of Relationships*. It will help you Pick Right.

14

CHAPTER 2

VITAL INGREDIENTS OF
A SUCCESSFUL RELATIONSHIP

VITAL INGREDIENTS OF A SUCCESSFUL RELATIONSHIP

A relationship, like any partnership, requires honesty and trust. You don't invest in a business, looking forward to being ripped off. Agreements must be kept, and truth must shine. The moment partners start to hide information, lie to each other or in any way violate the trust put in them, the partnership starts falling apart. Yet some people believe that romantic relationships are an exception, and they foolishly allow honesty to be compromised.

Honesty and trust are *vital* ingredients in a relationship. *Vital* means "necessary to life." Indeed, high levels of trust and honesty are *necessary to the life* of your relationship. They are so vital that they are part and parcel of the definition of the word itself.

A *relationship* could be defined as *a union that improves the lives of its members and is conducted with honesty.*

Being honest is not always easy. It takes courage. But honesty and courage are essential to a happy and fulfilling *life*! If you compare life to a pie, it is only as good as its ingredients. Poor ingredients make for a bad pie—and an inferior life.

So don't start a relationship with pretense or white lies, or any-color lies. Be yourself and be truthful. Don't change yourself to catch your match. If the supposed "right match" doesn't like you the way you are, then that person isn't the right match for you. Similarly, make sure that he or she is truthful with you. Lies are a red flag not to be ignored. And from the very start, establish an agreement that you'll be truthful with one another and will not betray each other's trust.

Betrayal of trust can be so fatal to a relationship that it can bring it to an abrupt end. It can even turn love into hate. Examples are all around us.

"Anyone who doesn't take truth
seriously in small matters cannot
be trusted in large ones either."
—Albert Einstein

WHEN THEY DON'T LOVE YOU ANYMORE

While on the subject of honesty, you need to know something about a relationship partner who, all of a sudden, "doesn't love you anymore." The person who, unexpectedly, is "no longer in love" has been dishonest. He or she has accumulated a pile of secrets that he or she will not reveal. Having been untruthful, the individual *suddenly* wishes to leave, excusing it with "I don't love you anymore."

When that happens, don't bother to soul-search hoping to understand your own faults. If you failed in any way, you failed to keep him or her honest.

So establish your relationship on a foundation of trust, honesty and integrity. These are ingredients you can't do without, because once they go out the window, so does the relationship.

ANOTHER INGREDIENT YOU CAN'T DO WITHOUT

Another vital ingredient is communication. It too is part of the definition of the word. A relationship could be further defined as *a union that improves the lives of its members and is conducted with honesty, and whose members maintain good communication with each other.*

You may recall a time when you had just met someone new. You talked up a storm, didn't you? You shared your thoughts and feelings. And you listened to one another.

Most couples start off with good communication. Then they figure, "We already know each other," and so they stop sharing quite as much or listening as well as they should. They get comfortable in the relationship. After all, they have already "acquired" each other. So from that point on, they make little effort to nurture their union. They put it "on automatic," believing that it will be there with no effort of their own. But instead, it weakens. They become less of a team. They grow apart.

Interestingly enough, this vital ingredient of *communication* is closely related to our previous ingredients of *honesty* and *trust*. Good communication cannot exist in the absence of honesty. Lies make it necessary to restrict what we say, so we can no longer communicate freely.

Have you ever done something wrong as a child? You knew that if you were found out you would be in trouble. So you couldn't talk about it. If you then kept accumulating secrets you felt you had to hide, I am sure you communicated less and less and distanced yourself from the people around you.

This common occurrence is the cause of communication breakdowns between relationship partners, between parents and children, and between friends and coworkers.

Be it spending more money than agreed or sleeping with another man or woman, the person tries to keep it a secret. His or her communication, which previously was open and free, is now restricted. The person starts to censor what he or she says and tries to remember what was said before. And so this individual communicates less and less, and the relationship starts to fall apart.

Without honesty, trust and open communication a relationship is doomed to fail. In Picking Right, find someone you can trust, and be yourself trustworthy. Then keep the communication between you open and strong, and your future will look bright.

> *"If you tell the truth, you don't*
> *have to remember anything."*
> —Mark Twain

WEIGH IT UP

Now that we have covered the most fundamental necessities of a successful relationship—honesty, trust and open communication— let's learn to assess any relationship on our journey of Picking Right.

Suppose you are facing a scale. On one side of it, place the joy and happiness your relationship brings: all your pleasurable moments together, the strength you both draw from your union, the support and empowerment you each get, the personal growth you have both experienced and any future promise.

On the other side of the scale place your moments of grief and pain, upset or betrayal of trust. Include any personal deterioration, such as lowered self-esteem or lessened accomplishments in life. And don't forget any potential trouble, such as that caused by drug use, excessive drinking or an inability to keep a job.

Now weigh it up—and be brutally honest with yourself. Is this relationship an asset or a liability? Is the "advantages side" heavier than the "disadvantages side?" It better be!

And since the word *advantage* comes from *advance*, ask yourself: *Is this relationship **advancing** your lives (both of you), or is it holding you back?*

The Relationship Assessment exercise at the end of this chapter will give you the skill of weighing it up. It will help you evaluate any relationship with great clarity.

Additionally, it could enable you to tip the scales. You know what a worthwhile relationship is now and what to measure: happiness, personal growth, improvement of life—any and all positive factors versus the negative. This assessment will pinpoint *what* about your relationship is positive and what must change.

With that in mind, you can work together to make the advantages outweigh the disadvantages by a great margin. And if you can do that, you have just *created* the Right Pick.

> *"A worthwhile relationship*
> *is a union that improves*
> *the lives of its members and*
> *is conducted with honesty."*
> —The Author

EXERCISE 2
Relationship Assessment:
Weighing It Up

Note: It is recommended that you fill in your answers on a
separate sheet of paper or make a copy of the next page.

Do this exercise concerning a current or past relationship. It will give you practice in assessing and evaluating any relationship. Additionally, if you are still upset about the loss of a relationship, this might help you get over it.

If you are currently in a relationship and have some doubt about it, this can help you make a decision. Or, if you wish to *better* the relationship you are in, you will gain insight as to what needs to change to bring about an improvement.

Consider the relationship carefully, and please be brutally honest with yourself. Place a check mark in the appropriate column for each of the ten points listed on the next page. Then add up the number of check marks in each column and enter the total.

While in this relationship I am (or was)...

	YES	SOMEWHAT	NO
Feeling better about myself	_____	_____	_____
More optimistic about life	_____	_____	_____
Feeling happier overall	_____	_____	_____
Having more self-respect	_____	_____	_____
Being more productive	_____	_____	_____
Having more self-confidence	_____	_____	_____
Pursuing my goals	_____	_____	_____
Feeling more ambitious	_____	_____	_____
Being more creative	_____	_____	_____
Building my future	_____	_____	_____
TOTAL:	_____	_____	_____

All "yes" is ideal. All "no" is bad. And there are many shades of gray in between.

Considering the above, would you say the relationship

Was helpful to you? ____

Did little for you? ____

Drained you? ____

Having done this exercise, you should have a better insight into relationships and a greater ability to assess and weigh up the pros and cons of any relationship. You can also predict how much work may be required to elevate a relationship toward the ideal and at what cost or sacrifice. Does it need minor fine-tuning or a thorough overhaul? How do the rewards compare with the efforts invested?

Every relationship is unique, and the way to find out the answers is by weighing it up.

CHAPTER 3

COMMON MISTAKES THAT COULD COST YOU YOUR HAPPINESS

CHAPTER 3

COMMON MISTAKES THAT COULD COST YOU YOUR HAPPINESS

Now that we've covered what a good relationship is supposed to be, some of its vital ingredients, and what it takes to create it, let's take a look at the pitfalls of trying to Pick Right. Let's see where we tend to go wrong so that we may avoid such pitfalls on our journey to the goal of having a healthy, happy, long-lasting relationship.

RELATIONSHIP MYTHS

A myth is a false idea that many people believe to be true. The word comes from Greek *mythos* meaning "a legend or story."

We have all been exposed to "legends" and "stories" about relationships, including some wild ideas regarding Picking Right. Let's examine some of these myths.

After all, it is truth that sets you free; and in this case, truth will empower you to pick the right person for you.

> *"You'll miss the best things*
> *if you keep your eyes shut."*
> —Dr. Seuss

ALL YOU NEED IS LOVE

A common myth we all grew up with is that love, all by itself, is a sound foundation for a relationship. How do we decide to start a relationship? We "fall in love."

> *"Gravitation is not responsible for people falling in love."*
> —Albert Einstein

EMOTIONS CAN BETRAY YOU

Emotions can be misleading. Often, feelings have little to do with whether or not a relationship can last or bring happiness.

Have you ever witnessed an abusive relationship? Emotions run high. "Love" is hotter than fire. Yet the outcome is misery for all concerned, as the following true-life story illustrates.

Sue was a single mother living with a physically abusive boyfriend. One day she found herself in jail! They had gotten in a heated argument, both called the police, and she was arrested.

After spending a few nights in jail she disappeared from sight. She'd been sent to a domestic violence shelter for forty-five days, along with her kids. Judges know that victims need a break from abusive "love" and hoped that a long break would help end the relationship.

When Sue returned to town, there was additional drama: the boyfriend attempted to sell her belongings, and friends and the police protected her while she moved her property out of his house.

You'd think that would have been the end of it. Not so. Sue went back to her boyfriend. She loved him, she said.

There is nothing wrong with love. It's a beautiful thing. It is necessary in a relationship, and in any good relationship it keeps growing. But while "in love" you still have to keep your eyes open or disaster will strike, as this next real-life story shows.

Amy and Greg met at a bar. She was cute, he was handsome, and they'd both had too much to drink. They laughed a lot together and sex was good, which seemed to them a perfect foundation for what turned into a marriage and a baby.

Not long into the relationship, Amy discovered that Greg had continued to pursue sexual thrills outside the home. In his world, he was not ready for a monogamous relationship. One wonders why he chose to get married and start a family.

The relationship was doomed to fail.

Several years of drama ensued. Greg refused to change his conduct, and Amy made his life miserable while still hoping he would reform. I suspect that even after their divorce she kept hoping he would turn into an angel and realize what a find she was. That never happened.

SHE WAS WRONG—TWICE

Amy's story is a lesson in Picking Wrong. She wanted to be married. She wanted to be a mother. Although her own relationship history was as wild as Greg's, she was ready to put it behind her and settle down.

Amy didn't discuss commitment with Greg prior to getting married. She did not ensure that his vision of their future was the same as hers. She *assumed* that their love had transformed him and that his marriage proposal was also a vow of fidelity.

The sad truth is most people have a behavior pattern. Anyone who would go home with you after a night in a bar has been going home with other people following a casual encounter. You must ask yourself: *Is he or she truly ready for a commitment or a change?* Often the person is not.

This doesn't mean that people cannot change—they can. But wouldn't you rather let a promiscuous person reform and *stabilize* in their new ethical life before you surrender your love and life to them? Attempting to reform your mate can turn into a disaster.

Amy's first mistake was to believe she was so special that Greg would promptly reform. That wouldn't have been so fatal had she avoided the second mistake: once she discovered Greg's infidelity, she *stayed* with him. The baby hadn't been born yet. This would have been the perfect time to wipe off her tears, chalk it up to experience and end the relationship. But she couldn't admit that she was wrong.

> *"You can't depend*
> *on your eyes*
> *when your imagination*
> *is out of focus."*
> —Mark Twain

THE "SOUL MATE"

Some couples refer to each other as "soul mates."

We think of a soul mate as someone who completes us, our other half; someone we "have to" be with. Unfortunately, such intense feelings are not guaranteed to bring happiness nor be a solid foundation for a successful relationship. Yet both men and women fall into the soul-mate trap.

What is a *soul mate*, and how might the soul-mate myth impact one's life? The following real-life stories shed light on this.

Paul was getting ready to marry his high school sweetheart, even though she had cheated on him on several occasions. His friends all tried to get him to open his eyes but to no avail. He was going to marry his "soul mate."

On their wedding day it rained cats and dogs. A morbid joke developed that even God was crying for Paul. They went through with the wedding. A year later Paul's wife was still cheating, while he grew fat and depressed.

* * *

Sara was a beautiful young woman of a humble beginning. She longed for happiness but she was young and naive. Carl was a seasoned womanizer. He pursued Sara until she was convinced that he was her soul mate.

On the morning after the wedding, his true nature came to light. He was rude, domineering and mean. He gave her no support in the face of his family's hostility. Her dreams of a loving husband and a happy family were shattered.

Still, she stayed. He was, after all, her "soul mate." Then children were born, and she believed herself to be trapped.

SOUL MATES ARE MADE, NOT FOUND

It is up to each couple to create the bond, trust, unity and affection that make them *mates of the soul*. Soul mates are *created*, not *found*.

A couple will find that they have to work consistently and continuously to nurture their union. A relationship is like a garden: If you neglect it, it withers. If you continually work at it, it blossoms.

A couple who start out as "soul mates" but find that, despite honest efforts, the relationship brings them nothing but grief, must question the validity of their union.

COMPROMISING

Sometimes "soul mates" stay in a bad relationship because each of them feels that their partner is the only person they can ever love. They might even believe that they can't do any better. Throughout their life they've been told that "everybody cheats" or that they should "learn to compromise." So they compromise on everything—big and small.

Compromising can be a mistake, depending on the size and nature of the matter. Some issues are subject to compromise because they are minor or even petty. Some have to do with character differences, which may be allowed for: suppose he likes to ride motorcycles, while she prefers to swim; or he likes action movies, and she can't stand them. Such differences are harmless. But the flagrant ones—like the woman who *knew* her husband was sexually abusing their daughters and did nothing about it? That is an "over-my-dead-body" issue. No compromise there!

A GOOD MATE IS HARD TO FIND

Another myth is that good people are rare. So couples compromise out of a sense of scarcity. They say, "I can't find anyone," "I've been single for too long," or "My biological clock is ticking." They have been convinced that mates are scarce or that all the good ones are taken.

Please realize that on a planet populated by over seven billion people, with roughly half of them of the opposite sex, there must be one decent person who is right for you! The truth is, there is more than one; because a relationship is a *creation*, much like a work of art. It isn't something that "happens" to you, but something that you and your mate *make happen* together.

A sense of scarcity is a dangerous mindset in *any* area of life. A person who believes that jobs are scarce could get stuck in a dull job and never follow his or her dreams. Believing that friends are scarce could lead to tolerating people who don't deserve your friendship. In relationships, a person will often endure tremendous abuse out of a sense of scarcity. So don't buy the scarcity myth. It is a dangerous lie.

BE TRUE TO YOUR DREAMS

Some would tell you that your goals are unattainable. That is a myth.

In relationships and in life as a whole, remember this: Your dreams are *your* dreams. You must have the courage to dream them and the perseverance to achieve them. Don't give up a dream because it doesn't materialize rapidly or because someone tries to discourage you. All worthwhile achievements take hard work.

You may have to spend many Saturday nights alone. So what? Put up with solitude and find something pleasant to do with friends, family or on your own. Help someone. Volunteer in the community. Become proud of your personal achievements and good works, all the while searching for your Right Pick.

Don't let your dreams get lost, diluted or compromised. You are more valuable than you've been led to believe, and you deserve to achieve your goals.

> *"Don't part with your illusions.*
> *When they are gone,*
> *you may still exist,*
> *but you have ceased to live."*
> —Mark Twain

EXERCISE 3
Relationship Myths

Note: It is recommended that you fill in your answers on a
separate sheet of paper or make a copy of these pages.

From a young age we have been exposed to false information,
and today relationship myths are all around us. It is important to
acknowledge such falsehoods for what they are. The purpose of this
exercise is to help you do just that.

RELATIONSHIP MYTHS

List some popular ideas, opinions or "facts" about men, women or
relationships that you know or suspect to be false.

_____

_____

_____

_____

COMPROMISING

List some issues or differences that you might be willing to compromise
on in your relationship.

_____

_____

_____

_____

List some issues or differences that are unacceptable to you and which you would refuse to compromise on in your relationship.

_____

_____

_____

A SENSE OF SCARCITY

Think back to a time or times when you or someone else compromised in a relationship out of a "sense of scarcity." What was the outcome?

_____

_____

_____

SOUL MATES

Recall a specific "soul mate" relationship that you witnessed or experienced that turned disastrous. What happened?

_____

_____

_____

Recall a specific "soul mate" relationship that you witnessed or experienced in which the partners made it that way.

_____

_____

_____

CHAPTER 4

*A*VOID THESE MISTAKES

CHAPTER 4

*A*VOID THESE MISTAKES

It is safe to say that no part of life gets as wild and crazy as relationships. And it all begins with failing to Pick Right.

Perhaps you know someone who has had a rough relationship history. If you've known them long enough to witness them getting in and out of relationships, you possibly noticed a pattern: they pick similar people and have similar problems with each one of them. It's almost as if they marry the same person over and over again: a different person but always the same *type*.

The man whose wife cheated on him takes a while to heal. When he finally does, he picks another cheater. At last he concludes that "all women cheat." Although such a conclusion doesn't equip him to build a better relationship in the future, it is comforting to have a firm opinion on the subject, even if it's false.

The truth is, there are warning signs that identify cheaters. He didn't know how to read the signs, so he Picked Wrong again—a different mate but the same type of person.

The following real-life stories provide some examples.

One businessman only dated actresses and model look-alikes and had trouble with each of them. The girlfriend he introduced to me was pretty nutty, and they had a lot of drama, but she surely fit his standards. However, because those standards had nothing to do

39

with Picking Right, he continued to go from one rocky relationship to the next.

* * *

An attractive professional kept picking abusive men. She would be intimidated by her men, support them financially and end up swindled and confused. Sadly, her three beautiful children from an abusive ex-husband were pulled into her drama through no fault of their own.

* * *

A beautiful girl kept falling for unattractive men who made her feel inadequate. Here was "Beauty" constantly anxious about her looks and seeking approval from the "Beast." But no sooner would she extract herself from one "Beast" than she would "fall in love" with another.

Different partners, same type.

WASTING YOURSELF ON THE WRONG PERSON

The ordinary course of a relationship goes from dating to steady dating, to commitment, to talks about the future, and so on. It develops in that fashion or it ends. However, when only one side desires a future together, this progression does not occur, and you see that person waiting in vain. If this is someone you love, it pains you to see them wasting themselves on the wrong person—someone who is not going to reciprocate and bring them the happiness they desire.

Here is but one of many examples that crossed my path.

Mary was an educated professional in her forties who was looking for the love that would lead her to the altar. John was a confirmed bachelor who made enough money to support extravagant dating and

40

who found no advantage in giving up decades of bachelorhood for marriage. Despite their conflicting relationship goals, they dated for several years.

Throughout their relationship, Mary doubted John's fidelity, and her suspicions were confirmed on more than one occasion with incriminating evidence. As their differences intensified, so did their conflicts.

Their breakup nearly killed Mary. She started drinking excessively and let her career go downhill. She was obsessed with John. Although she spied on him and saw him with new girlfriends, she was unable to put it behind her and move on. When she came to see me two years later, she had gained weight from daily wine intake and looked ten years older. By that time she had gone back to work and was making attempts at dating.

Then an unexpected phone call came in. John had reached out to her, and they spoke on the phone for hours. Mary's world turned upside down. She was ready to forgive everything. All she wanted was an apology and, in return, she would have given herself to him unconditionally.

Mary e-mailed me asking for my advice "as an expert and a friend." I replied:

"Dear Mary,

"I will tell you as an expert and especially as a friend—in fact, I will give you the advice I would give my own sister. Everything I'll say, you already know; otherwise, you wouldn't be asking my opinion.

"John wasn't good for you in the past. What makes you think he'll be good for you in the future? You will never get from him what you want: marriage, fidelity, the sharing of your lives and growing old

together. Not because you are not good enough, but because he is not honest enough.

"When a person has cheated and lied a lot, they can get trapped in their own behavior pattern. Most thieves don't reform. They keep stealing and going back to jail.

"You'll always have to share him with other women. He is not ready to be a one-woman man. He is in his fifties. Do you really think he'll change now? All a woman can expect of him is heartbreak. Not because he is God's gift to women, but because he is dishonest and won't commit.

"Your relationship with him almost took you to your grave. It turned you into an alcoholic. It almost drove you insane. Do you really want to take that chance again?

"Ask yourself: Do I want to live or die? Do I want to destroy myself or build myself back up?

"If you really feel that you are such a bad person, that you deserve more abuse, then go do some missionary work or save some lives until you feel that you deserve better, because this is an offer from the devil."

And I advised her to move on. I hope she did.

We make our choices, and the life we have is proof of whether or not we chose right.

It is a gross mistake to waste yourself on the wrong person. If someone cannot appreciate you the way you are, if they cannot return your love, your loyalty and devotion, you need to move on and find someone who will.

Remember that a relationship is not worth having unless it brings happiness and a better life to both of you. You need a mate who will appreciate you and want you in their life. If all you get is suffering and pain, what's the use? It's a Wrong Pick. You are wasting yourself and, indeed, your entire life.

> *"You can search throughout*
> *the entire universe for*
> *someone who is more deserving*
> *of your love and affection*
> *than you are yourself,*
> *and that person is*
> *not to be found anywhere.*
> *You, yourself, as much as anybody*
> *in the entire universe,*
> *deserve your love and affection."*
> —Buddha

THE ROLLER COASTER

Love is often used to justify putting up with abuse: "I know I'm miserable, but we love each other so much!"

In some strange way, the feeling called "love" is supposed to make up for being in an unhappy, unworthy relationship. The following real-life story is such an example.

Dan kept moving in and out of his girlfriend's house like a yo-yo. It was love one day and pack-up-your-bags-you-are-moving-out the next. Breakups came with verbal abuse on the order of "You are a zero," shortly to be followed by "I love you; please come back." And every time he went back.

If your relationship is a roller coaster of this kind, end it while it's still young. Extreme ups and downs signify a Wrong Pick. It means that the two of you provoke each other to destructive behavior—and ruined lives. You may be good people, each in his or her own right, but *together* you would eventually destroy the relationship and hurt each other.

Such a relationship is often passionate and fiery. "Make-up sex," they say, is good. However, the crash that follows can practically kill you.

Additionally, how can you build a bright future on the rocky foundation of unpredictable highs and lows? What you need is a gradual climb up, up, up, getting better bit by bit.

Life itself offers plenty of challenges, without the craziness of an unstable relationship. Your relationship should be a safe harbor, where you both find calm and support. It's the place to renew your strength before you head for the front line again to continue the battles of your life.

PHYSICAL AND VERBAL ABUSE

There is no justification for domestic violence. No woman or man in their right mind should tolerate it. Sometimes the people who do are substance abusers. Drugs and alcohol have the power to corrupt anyone's judgment and dramatically lower their standards. In such a case, the first step must be sobriety.

But how about a sober individual? How often do they justify and explain their partner's violence with ridiculous excuses?

Perhaps they forget that a human being is not a punching bag and shouldn't be treated like one. Force and violence add up to oppression. In the United States, slavery has long since been abolished. Why condone inhuman treatment in your own home?

While violence is physical force, *verbal abuse* is mental force. Telling someone that they are worthless, that they will never amount to anything, that their ideas are stupid, is cruel and unnecessary. It improves nothing. It degrades their thoughts, opinions and dreams. It is oppressive.

If verbal or physical abuse occurs early in your relationship, end it without regret. The abusive behavior is either typical of your new mate or the two of you provoke each other to mutual destruction. Most people try to be on their best behavior in the early stages of a relationship. If they can't control themselves early on, they aren't likely to do so later when they have you in their back pocket, so to speak.

PROBATION

When you first start a relationship, both of you are on probation. The word *probation* means "the testing or trial of a person's conduct, character, etc."

Like a new employee, your conduct, character and performance are put to the test. That's when you examine one another to see whether or not you are suitable for each other. During that time you should be most unforgiving about signs of trouble.

The following real-life story tells of someone who overlooked a flunked probation.

Karen and Ed were a new couple. After living together for about three weeks (he had moved in with her) and while out of town on business, Ed jumped into bed with another woman.

When Karen called me, sobbing, I said, "Dump him now! If he can't be faithful to you this early in the relationship, recognize who you are dealing with and move on!"

She wouldn't listen. A year later they got married, and two years afterwards they were divorced. By then Ed owed Karen a lot of money, and a few more years went by before she got paid back. This relationship was a complete waste of several years of her life, simply because she had overlooked a flunked probation.

A relationship partner who starts off with betrayal has flunked his or her probation. The early betrayal is a gross red flag you mustn't ignore. Here is plain evidence of poor moral values. You don't need a crystal ball to predict the future.

During the probation period people look out for signs: Is the prospective partner romantic? Does he or she treat me right? Are we having fun together? They may be impressed with education, career or financial status. They try hard to be optimistic and to stress the better side of their prospect.

While they might concern themselves with milder indications of character such as those mentioned above, they often undervalue flagrant warning signs, as did Karen.

Infidelity is a deal breaker. Due to HIV and other sexually transmitted diseases, it is also dangerous. This isn't a flaw you should forgive as an "accident." A mate who would betray you when the relationship is young and he or she is still eager to please is very likely to do so in the future.

Betrayal of trust doesn't occur only through infidelity. Gambling, excessive drinking and drug use are gross warning signs of future backstabbing. So are lies. Lying is an attempt to manipulate you. Any dishonesty or pretense is a betrayal, and you should not gloss over it.

THE BEST DEAL IS A NO DEAL

In one of his books, real estate tycoon Robert Allen teaches that sometimes *"the best deal is a no deal."* I am sorry to liken relationships to real estate. It isn't very romantic. But neither is divorce.

When it comes to Picking Right, sometimes the best relationship is a NO relationship! When a relationship brings much more pain than joy (and does not improve despite your best efforts), it just isn't worth it!

Here is a real-life example.

Phil and Beth's relationship was troublesome from the start. It began passionately; they got married, had a child. Their personalities made for a stormy union, with frequent ups and downs.

Beth caught Phil cheating on several occasions, but she believed in love and marriage. She kept hoping they would make it work.

They didn't. Phil eventually insisted on a divorce and their unhappy saga ended.

Was this relationship worth having? Was it worth fighting for? It brought both parties grief and pain, because it was the result of Picking Wrong. Furthermore, when a relationship goes sour, other parts of life are affected. Indeed, their respective careers suffered. Only after the divorce had been settled, and their relationship as divorced people had smoothed out, did their individual careers recover.

A bad relationship can be a great distraction from the attainment of goals and the enjoyment of life. It can even bring the rest of one's life to ruin.

CAN'T LET GO

Like Beth, many men and women have a hard time letting go. Emotions enter in and rational thinking becomes impossible. The pain and fear of loss hit like a powerful wave threatening to overwhelm them.

In that state of mind, they fail to see what they let go of when they make a "no deal" with someone who has betrayed them or otherwise flunked probation. They let go of potential misery; of disrespect, mental and emotional abuse; of someone who obviously considers them unimportant, if not worthless.

If a relationship is wrong, it is wrong. Insisting that it is right, when it isn't, does no good.

Failed relationships have been known to result in failed lives! Anyone who would have a negative effect on you isn't worth having in your life.

Life is ahead of you. The past is history. As long as you are alive, you can create a future for yourself. Every moment you waste clinging to a low-grade relationship is precious time you can spend finding and creating your ideal one.

The coming chapters and their exercises provide tools you can use to overcome and triumph.

> *"You cannot make yourself feel*
> *something you do not feel,*
> *but you can make yourself do right*
> *in spite of your feelings."*
> —Pearl Buck

EXERCISE 4
Trusting Your Own Judgment

Most people don't give themselves all the credit they deserve; you may be one of those people. Yet deep inside, you know what is right for you, what your dreams are, your goals, your vision.

Still, how often have you been encouraged or even convinced to compromise that vision? Perhaps you didn't trust your own judgment enough and believed that others knew better. Only after the fact did you realize that you were right in the first place and wished you had taken your own advice.

The purpose of this exercise is to boost your confidence in your own judgment, as it relates to relationships, and increase your trust in yourself, which may have been lowered by mistakes or failures.

A WORD OF CAUTION

While doing this exercise, you may suddenly recall all the mistakes you have ever made. Disregard them. We want to highlight the times when you made the *correct* relationship decisions (or at least knew what they were even if you failed to act on them). You may find that you were right more often than you suspected.

EXERCISE

1. Recall a specific time when you made a decision about a relationship and the outcome proved that you were right.

2. Recall a specific time when you made a decision about a relationship but were convinced to change your mind. The final outcome proved that you were right in the first place and should have taken your own advice.

3. Recall a specific time when you made a decision about a relationship and acted on it despite others' efforts to convince you otherwise. The final outcome proved that you were right after all.

Recall several of each. Or cycle through them: 1, 2, 3, 1, 2, 3, etc.

If you can't recall an example of one of the above, move on to the next one. Keep cycling through the three steps until you feel better than you did when you first started this exercise.

You may now find that you feel more confident in your ability to make correct decisions about relationships or even about life as a whole.

* * *

This exercise is empowering and can be done again and again in the future. Whenever you feel a need for a confidence boost, do it again. As your faith in your own judgment increases, you will make better and better decisions.

Ultimately, all the truth you will ever find is within you!

"Truth is by nature self-evident.
As soon as you remove
the cobwebs of
ignorance that surround it,
it shines clear."
—Mahatma Gandhi

CHAPTER 5

DETECTING TROUBLE BEFORE IT STARTS

CHAPTER 5

DETECTING TROUBLE BEFORE IT STARTS

Old habits are hard to break. Indeed, most people have behavior patterns that rarely change. Your first clue to someone's true nature and what you should expect of them in the future is their "history"— how and what they have been doing before you met them. Their past behavior predicts the challenges you may face in the future.

HISTORY REPEATS ITSELF

Often the writing is on the wall, but we refuse to read it. We ignore the signposts, which clearly announce *Serious Issues, Can't Commit, Addiction, Freeloader, Unreliable* or simply *Can't make up his or her mind.*

The person we date may try to warn us of the danger they pose to us. It's as if they wish to protect us from themselves. They may even mistreat us to make us leave. We must observe their current behavior as well as consider their past. What picture unfolds? What are we really getting ourselves into?

And we must be *honest* with ourselves about it. No rose-colored glasses allowed!

Your relationship shouldn't be a reformation process. Yes, creating harmony between you takes work, but your issues shouldn't be so extreme that you spend your life trying to change your mate. In the first place, it is often a losing battle. And secondly, you wouldn't want someone constantly trying to change and "improve" *you*.

So find a partner who is suitable for you, who has similar standards and goals, and build a life where you both may thrive. Like two graceful dancers, you must be in sync with one another—not constantly step on each other's toes. Relationships that begin with too big a struggle to make a square peg fit in a round hole don't promise a happy, harmonious future.

And remember: there are *billions* of people on Earth. If you don't waste your life on the Wrong Pick, you'll increase your chances of finding the right person for you.

DON'T BE GULLIBLE

The following applies to any interpersonal relationship, not only a romantic one. Be forewarned that these may be hard facts to swallow, but they are true and could save your life, happiness and sanity.

Truth isn't always popular, but that doesn't make it less of a truth. Writing about it might do little for my popularity, but I write to better my readers' lives, not for praise.

Don't be gullible or naive.

If someone is dishonest, their deception spills over from one area of life to the next. It's their behavior pattern across the board: Poor integrity in business signifies similar standards in interpersonal relationships. It's how they treat the people in their life.

Observe their behavior, and don't sugarcoat it with how they *had* to lie to their boss or friend but they are, without a shadow of a doubt, honest with you.

The truth is, if they are deceitful, it is only a matter of time before they deceive you.

This is hard for most people to accept. The following real-life example is only too typical.

Joanne was trying to help a girlfriend who was going through a divorce. When she told me that the reason for the divorce was her friend's extramarital affairs, I advised her to stay away from this "friend." Her friend's disloyalty as a wife defined her character; and it was only a matter of time before her dishonesty would spill over and affect the rest of the people in her life, including Joanne, who was trying to help her. Joanne wouldn't hear of it, of course.

I haven't seen Joanne for several years now; I sometimes wonder whatever happened to this friendship. Because you don't need a crystal ball to predict someone's future behavior. All you need to do is inspect their past.

We see this in people who date a married person. The fatal mistake they make is to believe that the person would change once he or she became "theirs." They fall for stories of mistreatment by the other spouse—how misunderstood and unhappy this married person has been. *"Obviously,"* they naively think, *"their terrible home life justifies their affair with me. But I am their Right Pick and with me they'll be different."*

No they won't, as this next real-life story demonstrates.

Jim and Tracy started their relationship while both were married to other people. They dismantled their respective homes—children and all—for the sake of their newfound "love" and wound up in a disastrous marriage: constant conflicts, mutual accusations and general unhappiness.

Some years later I met Jim. When he bitterly complained about Tracy, I immediately asked if he was unfaithful to her. (Criticism and faultfinding are sure signs of guilt for one's wrongdoing. More on that later.) *Jim admitted that he'd been having affairs. In fact, he'd been doing to Tracy exactly what he had done to his first wife.*

Old habits die hard and moral standards seldom change.

If you think that you deserve an honest person, then find one who *is*. Don't fool yourself into believing that you could pick a wolf and transform it into an innocent lamb.

> **"Morality is the basis of things
> and truth is the substance
> of all morality."**
> —Mahatma Gandhi

BUT CAN'T PEOPLE CHANGE?

I don't imply that people never change. In fact, as a Life Coach I help people daily to change their lives; to discontinue destructive patterns and establish constructive ones; to increase their ability to learn, to communicate and reach success; and to gain wisdom and tools that help them build the life and have the relationships they've always wanted. I have seen people change before my very eyes!

Furthermore, people have been known to change by going to church or temple, by moving to a different part of the country or by getting an education. A person can even change simply by *deciding* that he or she has had enough, and that from now on things will be different, as the following real-life example illustrates.

Joe spent from youth to adulthood as a gang member, involved in crime, drugs and violence. Nothing changed him: a devoted mother, the justice system, three divorces and children from four different women. Until one day he found himself facing serious legal trouble. This was too much even for him. Life finally got to him, and he decided to reform. He took a vow: If he gets off the hook this time, he will leave his life of crime and become a decent citizen.

Joe got a lucky break and kept his promise, never to return to his old ways.

So of course people *can* change, but not without a loud wake-up call.

A relationship, however, is not the place to force change. It is unfair to marry someone and hope that they'll change: If you don't like what you've got, don't marry it. If you want a skinny person, don't marry a fat one and spend your married life criticizing them for being overweight. If the person needs reform, let them go elsewhere to reform. Let life reform them. Don't marry them and then wish that they were different. You knew what you married, didn't you?

If the person's moral standards call for an upgrade, you are taking a chance. Even if they've been trying to reform and promise you that they have, do you really want to be the guinea pig on whom they practice their new values? Why waste your love, life and all you have to give on someone who might not repay you in kind?

Who made you believe that people are so scarce that you must settle for less? Perhaps it was someone who wasted their own life trying to reform the unreformable. Whatever the reason, you don't have to make the same mistake.

If you are decent, you deserve a decent mate. Your Right Pick is out there and you can find him or her, but only as long as you don't waste yourself on the wrong one.

"A round man cannot be expected
to fit in a square hole right away.
He must have time
to modify his shape."
—Mark Twain

DETECTING TROUBLE

How many times have you told yourself, *I should have known?*
You saw it coming, but you didn't have the courage to call a spade
a spade. It meant making decisions you didn't want to make,
so you ignored the red flags and defended your right to stay in a
substandard relationship.

We all know how "love" can end because someone didn't think
ahead. In the absence of foresight, romantic dreams shatter—be it
through unwillingness to commit, abuse, infidelity, addiction, neglect
of children, laziness or poor handling of finance.

The very issues we compromised on at the start come back to
haunt us and make us fail.

So why not think ahead? Why fool ourselves that the alcoholic
will stop drinking or the cheater will stop cheating, if we only "keep
an eye" on him or her?

And let's face it: if we have to keep an eye on the person, we are
already in trouble!

THE WRONG PICK

Most people wish to help. They seek to help their family, friends and
relationship partner. They try to do the right thing. They strive to
make their presence felt by contributing to their loved ones' lives. So
much so, that some even *stay* in miserable relationships because they

haven't given up on helping their mate. You may have known such people or may have done so yourself.

Unfortunately this is not true of everyone. There are people who are abusers, betrayers and backstabbers. Fortunately they are in the minority.

While being a minority, they bring about the majority of devastation. Therefore, we must know how to identify them and so preserve our hearts, health and happiness.

If based on your past experience it appears that "everyone" in the relationship world is a backstabbing abuser, then you must pay particular attention to the next chapter. It means that you have a tendency to fall into such people's webs, and that you tend to do so again and again.

What you need is the knowledge and tools to identify them—from a mile away—and never fall in their trap again.

What are the telltale signs that someone may be a backstabber and a Wrong Pick? The next chapter describes those signs and more.

EXERCISE 5
Detecting Trouble

Note: It is recommended that you fill in your answers on a
separate sheet of paper or make a copy of these pages.

Before you continue reading, let's review some of the tools introduced
in the last chapter, as they are vital in helping you Pick Right.

ARE THEY TRUSTWORTHY?

1. Do you know someone who has similar moral standards (high
or low) in several areas of their life, such as work, relationships,
responsibility for children, etc.? Describe.

_____

_____

_____

_____

2. Have you ever known someone who seemed to have different
moral standards in different areas of life? Describe. In your opinion,
is this person trustworthy?

_____

_____

_____

_____

CAN PEOPLE CHANGE?

1. Have you ever known someone who truly reformed or changed for the better? How did they accomplish this?

_____

_____

_____

_____

2. Do you know someone who *appeared* or *pretended* to have changed but had not? What effect did that have on the people in his or her life?

_____

_____

_____

_____

CHAPTER 6

*T*ELLTALE SIGNS

CHAPTER 6

*T*ELLTALE SIGNS

Following are key signs you must watch for. These are telltale signs that we notice but often choose to ignore. If we looked deeper, we might discover the "Oh my God!" truth that may be a deal breaker.

Suppose you hear a knock in your car engine. You could overlook it and get on the road, only to be stranded in the middle of nowhere. Or you could investigate it fully, discover the truth behind the knock and then determine whether or not your vehicle is ready for the trip you are about to take (or the commitment you are about to enter).

The following telltale signs are your relationship "knocks in the engine."

THE LIAR

Although lying has been mentioned earlier, it should be covered further, because we have a tendency to make less of it, to "understand" and forgive it. We try not to judge lying harshly because we have all lied before. If we criticize others, then we have to criticize ourselves as well. And that hurts.

However, when you catch your prospective mate in lies (whether he or she is lying to you or to someone else), you are confronted with a truly bad sign. Building a relationship with someone you can't trust is like constructing a house on thin air with no foundation to hold it down.

It is important to know that some people cover lies artfully. They can be so convincing! A drug user, for instance, could be talking to family over the phone, swearing up and down that they've been sober, while sticking a needle in their arm. It has been known to happen, and the first person to believe it—hook, line and sinker—is Mom.

Although liars may be hard to detect, they can still be identified. The "facts" they present do not add up; they don't totally make sense. While truthful information, like the pieces of a jigsaw puzzle, fits together, untruth does not.

Here is a simple real-life example.

Frank couldn't find a job for many months. His wife was puzzled: Was it the economy? Did something happen to the job market in their local area? Every day she would return home from work hoping for good news, but his story was always the same: he had been out job hunting but there were no jobs. Something didn't add up.

One day she discovered that Frank had been lying to her. He hadn't been job hunting at all. Although he left the house for several hours each day, he would visit friends or go to the mall, but he did not spend any time seeking employment.

Suddenly everything made sense, and the truthful (though unpleasant) facts added up.

The fact that some people lie should not lead you to suspect honest people. Most individuals try to be honest. As long as we show tolerance and don't lose our temper over every misunderstanding, they should feel safe to be truthful with us.

In the case of a child who accidentally breaks an object, he or she must feel safe to confess rather than hide the evidence. Parents who make telling the truth dangerous wind up raising liars.

THE CHEATER

As noted earlier, a person who has been promiscuous or perverted is liable to persist in their behavior pattern. Be forewarned and don't be shocked if you find yourself on the cheated end of the stick.

This person may have reformed, but don't trust them if it happened recently. Even if they swear that they've changed, give it some time. Don't make yourself a part of their experiment, and don't attempt to change them yourself. If you are the faithful type, then you deserve to be treated in kind.

Beginning a relationship with someone who is already in one is foolish. This person is cheating to be with you. They are obviously untruthful. They are leading a double life. They are confused. They may tell you how wonderful and special you are and how awful their mate or spouse is, which you want to believe. But remember that you may not be the first person they've cheated with and, most likely, not the last. They are a can of worms. Stay away.

THE FAKE

An insincere person is a detriment to any relationship. They are a fake, pretending to be someone or something they are not. "Hypocritical" describes them well. *Hypocrisy* comes from Greek, meaning "play the part." Indeed, they do. Like actors on a stage, they play the part they think will get them what they want.

If you see them treat someone a certain way and then turn around and talk about that person behind their back, don't think you are going to be an exception. If they do this to others, they'll do it to you. You will find that, while appearing to be on your side, they will injure you secretly.

Additionally, they may appear to be caring, warm and friendly. A deeper inspection will prove otherwise, as the following story illustrates.

Jason brought his new girlfriend home for the first time. She was beautiful, animated, charming and friendly. His mother found it odd that, throughout dinner, the conversation revolved around her. Not once did she turn to ask about anyone else in the room.

Then she received an important phone call and, within minutes, put everybody to work helping her explore a new career opportunity.

Although she pretended to be a "nice" and caring person, she was clearly self-centered, and the man she married would forever serve her needs and march to the beat of her drum.

She was a fake. Her friendly attitude was but a show that masked her true nature.

Again, such people are a minority, but that doesn't make them less of a liability. When love is young and the person good looking, it's easy to be blind to the facts. But *look* and you will recognize them.

> *"A man wrapped up in himself*
> *makes a very small bundle."*
> —Benjamin Franklin

THE NEGATIVE PERSONALITY

Do you know someone who always talks about how bad and dangerous things are? How you can't trust anybody and should always be careful? When somebody tries to do something new or take a chance, they immediately warn them of the risks. You start off sharing some bright idea with them, only to be filled with self-doubts by the end of the conversation.

They find negativity in everything.

Such a person brings up bad news, complains about how bad people and things are, gossips, criticizes and finds fault with others. You leave their company feeling that the world is not as safe or friendly as you had hoped, and that perhaps you are a fool for reaching high or for liking people. You start to doubt your abilities and strengths.

You will find that they awaken every fear you've been trying to overcome. Before you know it, you become as negative and cautious as they want you to be. "For you own good," they clip your wings and make sure you don't fly.

The negative personality is a Wrong Pick, particularly if you are an ambitious individual and have big dreams. With him/her, you will find it practically impossible to realize your full potential. If, on the other hand, you aren't naturally ambitious or have insecurities, this person will keep you weak and make you grow even weaker.

The Right Pick is a cheerleader. He or she provides encouragement when times are tough and applause whenever you triumph.

THE FICKLE TYPE

Have you ever met someone you could describe as irresponsible, capricious, flighty or fickle? The word *fickle* comes from Old English for *deceitful*. And indeed, such people are misleading.

You never know what to expect of them. They keep changing their minds. They won't stay on a given course. They start on a project with great vigor and, partway there, abandon it in favor of the next great thing. They start relationships with intense romance and cool down unexpectedly, causing heartbreaks and confusion.

Your relationship with this person might look promising one day and hopeless the next. This plays with your emotions. When they break a promise, they have an artful way of getting you to forgive them or even to believe that you were "making a big deal out of nothing." It is this "yo-yo effect" that keeps you hoping and wasting your love and life.

So watch for signs of fickleness. It is a telltale sign you don't want to ignore.

THE ADDICT

Drugs should be a big red flag to you. Under that banner there are "legal drugs" (prescriptions), illicit drugs ("street drugs"), as well as excessive drinking (alcohol *is* a drug).

Here is a telltale sign that the person is running away from something. Under the promising surface there are issues they can't face or negative emotions they are hoping to "drown" with their substance of choice.

More importantly, all substances are habit forming. In most cases, addiction itself becomes a greater problem than the issues that started it. And the drugs have severe side effects—physiological, mental and emotional.

For instance, alcohol is a depressant. Excessive use may result in depression, along with unreasonable hostilities and resentments toward others.

Amphetamine-type drugs (stimulants), including prescription stimulants, have side effects such as depression, hostility and paranoia. They have been known to induce insanity. (Paranoia itself is a mental illness that could result in violent acts done in delusionary "self-defense.")

Antidepressants are reported to cause sexual problems, anxiety, agitation and suicidal thoughts and behavior.

Less dramatic, yet detrimental to a relationship, is the lack of motivation and drive caused by habitual marijuana use, not to mention withdrawal symptoms, which include irritability, anxiety and aggression.

Who is going to be most affected by all this turmoil but the person closest to the user, their mate?

Don't fall for *"A little bit is okay," "It's an herb,"* or *"The doctor prescribed it."* Any mind-altering substance is a potential hazard to your relationship and life.

And don't be fooled because they "promise to stop." While most users don't want to be addicts, they are trapped in the vicious cycle of addiction. They are slaves to their substance and can't keep their promise. Without effective drug treatment, all they can offer you is heartache and disappointment. You could expect lying, cheating, infidelity, laziness, lack of ambition, stealing, failures at work and legal trouble, not to mention overdose and possible death.

Choose a sober mate or, if you must, send them to effective drug treatment. And then don't relax until they *are* sober.

With the growing rate of drug use (prescription and otherwise) facilities exist today that get users off medication, alcohol and other drugs safely. Many physicians and even some psychiatrists now specialize in weaning users off drugs on an outpatient basis, while utilizing nutritional supplements to assist in the process. In consulting such facilities and physicians, it is necessary to ensure that their goal is a drug-free patient, not someone whose old addiction is replaced with a "better drug." You may consult the resources section at the end of this book for further information.

Needless to say, it takes two to create a happy relationship. To be yourself a wonderful mate, you too must be sober. This may be an unpopular piece of advice in this tipsy, drugged, medicated society of ours. But I'd be remiss in my duties if I advised you otherwise. I have seen too much substance-related misery to sugarcoat this vital issue.

IMBALANCE OF GIVE AND TAKE

A good relationship is mutually beneficial, and the give and take are somewhat balanced. One couple had it worked out this way.

She made most of the income, while he took care of the pets, cooked, did the housework and chores, and was at her beck and call to assist and support her. This worked out for them and they enjoyed a good relationship.

Whatever the agreement, a couple should be helping one another and have a healthy balance of give and take. Neither one should be only receiving and doing little in return, or only giving and receiving nothing back.

Life could be likened to a journey whereby together you pull your carriage along many roads. You don't want to travel carrying your mate on your back, nor should your mate carry you on theirs. Rather, you should both contribute equally to pulling the carriage.

Surely, life presents illness and other challenges that may force one of you to carry the load for a stretch. That's where loyalty and devotion come in, and they are vital in any worthwhile relationship. But that would be the exception rather than the rule. The Right Pick would want to recover from his or her disability and get back in the game pulling the carriage along with you.

Naturally, you wouldn't treat the "balance" issue like a bank ledger: *"I did such and such while he or she did such and such. So who has a higher balance?"* The idea is that your mate does his or her best to contribute to you and is there for you in time of need, and vice versa.

If, however, your Pick is a sponge for help and service and does little to help you; if your life becomes consumed with helping and catering to this person, that is a telltale sign of trouble. You may be looking forward to a life of living *for* them rather than *with* them.

EXERCISE 6
Identifying Telltale Signs

Note: It is recommended that you fill in your answers on a
separate sheet of paper or make a copy of these pages.

Because people often ignore telltale signs of relationship trouble, it is
necessary to train ourselves to notice and acknowledge them.

The purpose of this exercise is to increase your ability to recognize
such signs and, when you do, remember to not explain them away.

EXERCISE

List some instances when you witnessed the following telltale signs.

The Liar

_____

_____

_____

The Cheater

_____

_____

_____

The Fake

_____

_____

_____

The Negative Personality

_____

_____

_____

The Fickle Type

_____

_____

_____

The Addict

_____

_____

_____

Imbalance of Give and Take

_____

_____

_____

CHAPTER 7

TYPES OF PEOPLE

*T*YPES OF PEOPLE

*H*ave you ever helped someone successfully? (It felt good, didn't it?) Conversely, have your efforts to help ever come to nothing? Perhaps some person was in dire straits, yet no matter how hard you tried, you were ineffective. It's as though they were a victim of life, and all your good intentions and sincere, hard work couldn't change that.

Some individuals seem to play the "victim game," and good people are drawn to them out of a desire to help. The victim might have had a rough life, and the world might have been cruel to him or her. But a victim personality is still a red flag.

THE VICTIM

The truth is, every one of us makes his or her bed and sleeps in it. Life doesn't just "happen" to us. Through the choices we make today, we take an active part in creating our tomorrow.

We take a job in a company. The company later goes bankrupt and we are out of a job. While it isn't our fault that the company folded, we chose to work there in the first place, didn't we? To that degree, we created our present condition as an unemployed person.

This doesn't mean that we chose wrongly. Our decision was right at the time we made it. It was based on the information at hand:

the company was stable and no one had a crystal ball to predict its future. So the outcome of being unemployed is not our *fault*, but we were still *responsible* for bringing it about.

The "victim" who makes you feel sorry for them and wakes up your desire to "save" them has done their share in making the bed they sleep in. Don't for a moment believe otherwise. However, they refuse to see how they may have brought it about or what they may have done to get themselves in the unfortunate position they are in.

There is a lot of talk about domestic violence, and many organizations help its victims. Yet most battered women are responsible, not only for choosing their abusers, but for *staying* with them and—the shocking part—for *returning* to them of their own free will. They are victims and, like the rest of us, take part in causing their misfortune.

A DIRTY WORD

The word *responsibility* is unpopular because it is associated with being at fault. However, there is a world of difference between *responsibility* and *fault*.

One dictionary definition sheds light on this matter. It says that someone who is *responsible* for something is *"the author or cause"* of it. And so, without feeling that an undesirable condition is our "fault," we can see that we took part in bringing it about.

This is a helpful approach because it says that we aren't the helpless victims of our fate but can do something to guide our destiny and, hopefully, build a better life. And if in addition to that we aren't obsessed with "being right" and aren't too hard on ourselves, then we can take responsibility for anything we "author" or are the "cause" of without getting overly serious about it.

"If I had no sense of humor,
I would long ago have committed suicide."
—Mahatma Gandhi

WHAT ARE THEY DOING ABOUT IT?

This is the next thing you want to take into consideration: Suppose someone *has* had a rough life, the true test is, are they doing anything to improve their lot?

A dynamic person will use the misfortunes of the past as valuable lessons to build a better future and will thrive in spite of all. Holocaust survivor Lucy Deutsch is such an example.

At the age of fourteen Deutsch was brought into the Nazi concentration camp Auschwitz. There, she says, she "encountered that infamous creature Dr. Mengele," also known by his nickname Angel of Death, which he earned for his inhumane experimentation on camp inmates, including children.

In spite of all she had been through, and losing her entire family during the war, Deutsch went on to become a successful business owner, novelist, screenwriter, songwriter and playwright. She got married and had children and grandchildren.

Still vital and creative at the age of 82, she produced a musical of her autobiography titled No Time to Weep. *An obviously remarkable individual, she says, "I hope my creative drive and determination can be an inspiration to others."*

So consider the person in front of you: Do they dwell on their past misery? Do they use it to gain sympathy or favors? Do they utilize their past failures to explain why they might fail in the future, rather than do something to change their luck?

If so, they aren't a Right Pick for you. They will always be a bundle of complaints and a sponge for help. You may feel strongly attracted to the challenge of salvaging them, but stay away. Even if you save their life, they will one day—after they've used you up—tell people how you've done them wrong. They are, after all, victims. They can't see their own responsibility in anything that happens to them. And they'll continue to play the victim game.

> *"He that won't be counseled*
> *can't be helped."*
> —Benjamin Franklin

THE PEOPLE IN YOUR MATE'S LIFE

Some people seem to be surrounded by happy, healthy friends and relatives. Everyone who comes into contact with them appears to be empowered, to feel and do better. People who befriend them or appeal to them for help do better as a result. They are almost magical in their effect on others. Like a green-thumbed gardener, they help every life they touch.

Have you ever known such an individual? That's the type of person you want in your life! By their side, you too will blossom.

On the other hand, there is the person whose friends and family do poorly in life. They get sick often; they have problems, accidents and "bad luck." It's as if this individual has a negative influence on his surroundings. Some might even call this "bad energy."

Have you ever known such a person?

Beware, because if you "plant" yourself around negative energy, in a garden tended by a bad gardener, you too will turn into a wilted flower.

Sounds mystical? Perhaps it is. Observe for yourself and see if you find this to be true. Then act accordingly.

AFFECTION

Some people are more demonstrative than others. If one mate has a great need to give and receive affection while the other is "cold," unhappiness may result. This is not as serious a red flag as some of the others.

It could be resolved by the less-demonstrative mate making an effort to display affection, and/or by the demonstrative mate working to become less sensitive. Remember, he or she has picked you. That in itself says *I love you.*

A word of advice to the demonstrative mate: Whenever you find your feelings easily hurt, ask yourself: *Am I tired or hungry?* You will find that you become touchy or irritable when your body is not at its best. Illness, tiredness, hunger, physical pain or discomfort can alter one's view of life and make everything appear very, very serious.

Ladies, take hormonal changes into consideration. That's when minor issues look bigger than they would if you were truly well. So, some parts of the month don't make an ideal time for deep discussions. Late nights, empty stomachs and illness never do either.

As for the less demonstrative mate, try to be thoughtful. A single hug or a tender word could bring harmony and cooperation with minimal effort on your part. And the benefit will be yours.

EXERCISE 7
Recognizing Red Flags

Note: It is recommended that you fill in your answers on a
separate sheet of paper or make a copy of the next page.

Most people are *able* to detect red flags but many are *unwilling* to
do so. You may have known someone who was perfectly capable of
hard work and could have been successful but was unwilling to get
into action. Without the willingness to exercise an ability, that ability
is useless.

The obvious reason people ignore red flags in relationships is
"hopeful thinking." They *want* to believe that their date is the Right
Pick and so go on disregarding obvious danger signals. There is
another reason though.

Consider this: Have you ever been discouraged from judging?
Have you ever been told that you were "too hard" on someone or
that you shouldn't be so "judgmental"? And have you ever taken such
advice, only to regret it later?

This is a common occurrence, which can wear down one's
willingness to judge. Without judgment, red flags can go unnoticed
and Picking Right becomes impossible.

The purpose of this exercise is to increase your *willingness* to
recognize red flags and to help you identify them early, before you
have invested too much time in the Wrong Pick.

EXERCISE

Choose a relationship you wish to assess. It may be a current or past relationship, yours or someone else's. On a piece of paper, list any "red flags" you have noticed and any additional ones you recognized some time later.

Relationship _____

List red flags you've noticed.

_____

_____

_____

List additional red flags you recognized some time later.

_____

_____

_____

How did the relationship end up?

_____

_____

Assess several relationships using this exercise until you feel that you can recognize red flags and correctly judge any relationship.

CHAPTER 8

WHY WE IGNORE THE RED FLAGS

WHY WE IGNORE THE RED FLAGS

While reading this book you may have recalled your own experiences or some drama from the lives of other people. Often, there is an *"I should have known!"* that comes after the fact, usually too late.

Why do we ignore the red flags? How come we refuse to see the obvious signs?

The answer is *fear*—fear of consequences or, more precisely, fear of the conclusions we might draw and the actions we might have to take.

If a man can't face calling the wedding off after catching his fiancée cheating, he might convince himself that it was an "accident"; that she didn't love the other guy; that "it meant nothing" to her because he is the one she really loves, and so on—whatever she sweet-talks him into believing.

Years later he would admit, *"I shouldn't have ignored those bright red flags."* But right when it happens he'd rather accept her justifications, forgive her, and name the problem something other than what it is.

When we refuse to face the truth, we have chosen to be blind. And being blind, we *will* fail to Pick Right.

WHAT'S A GIRL/GUY TO DO?

There is only one thing you can do about the red flags: Do NOT ignore them! And don't explain them away either. Explanations are just a way of saying that an obvious warning sign doesn't mean what you *know* it means. And explanations, more correctly labeled "excuses," improve nothing.

One woman "explained" her alcoholism to me. She said that her parents' divorce when she was a young child was at fault. That caused her alcoholism, she said. However, since there was nothing she could do to change her childhood, there was nothing she could do to become sober.

This was a plausible explanation, but utterly useless, because she continued to drink herself into bad health and a broken life.

We see similar irrationality happening all around us in relationships. How would you explain the situation of a husband who spends years in extramarital affairs, finally finds himself facing a divorce and *then* crawls back begging for forgiveness? What was he thinking? Did he really believe that he could get away with it? Was he that stupid? Obviously he was. If you must have an explanation, that will suffice.

Still some people are desperate to "understand" the illogical and "make sense" of the senseless. They might accept that the root of the problem was his "tough childhood" or some such nonsense. But since nobody's life gets any better with such an "understanding," it must be faulty. It certainly is a waste of time!

When it comes to Picking Right, you want the kind of understanding (not excuses or "explanations") that will help you build a happy, long-lasting relationship.

Do not ignore red flags, and don't fail to act on what they tell you.

THE BIGGEST MISTAKE

The biggest mistake we make in trying to Pick Right is that we tend to doubt ourselves. We see what we see, we notice the red flags, but are afraid to judge. We listen to what someone else has to say and discount our own observations. We think that they must know better, that we are probably wrong, that we should be more understanding or forgiving.

The following real-life stories are not uncommon.

Dena was paying the bills. Her boyfriend talked about the "big deals" he had in the works, while she kept supporting them. Dena needed to stop listening to the stories and start looking in her check register — the evidence was right there.

* * *

Harry caught his girlfriend in a lie. There was no need to sugarcoat it because "she didn't mean it" or it was a "small lie." It may be a small lie today and a big one tomorrow. It's a red flag.

LOOK! OBSERVE! NOTICE!

In order to make correct decisions, you must ask yourself: *What actually happened? What have I observed? What do I see?* Never deny what you yourself have observed, and don't listen to explanations of how what you observed wasn't really what you observed. Don't accept reasons why offensive conduct is acceptable. Instead of listening to what others say, *look* with your eyes wide open and decide for yourself how *you* view the situation.

There are exercises in this book that will help increase your trust in your own judgment. In relationships and in life as a whole, you are probably right more often than you give yourself credit for.

CLEARING YOUR MIND

Some relationships are so involved and confusing, you can't think clearly. There is so much bad in them, yet so much good, that you can't draw conclusions or make clear-cut decisions.

If you feel confused, don't sit at home trying to figure it out. Don't talk to friends for hours on end, absorbing everybody else's confusions and advice. The truth is, *you know what you should do.* Deep inside, *you know what is right.* You just need to clear your mind so that you can see it clearly.

One effective way to gain clarity is to go for long walks. But you must *look around you* while walking. Don't stay "in your head" and *think*, but *look* at things in your environment. Go for walks day after day, if you must, until you have a clear view of your situation. Then make your decision and act accordingly.

For precise instructions see Exercise 8, "Gaining Clarity," at the end of this chapter.

> *"Drag your thoughts*
> *away from your troubles...*
> *by the ears, by the heels,*
> *or any other way*
> *you can manage it."*
> —Mark Twain

EXERCISE 8
Gaining Clarity

This is a simple but powerful exercise.

If your life is going well, it will invigorate and empower you further. You may find that you become more creative and that you develop a "longer fuse" to deal with interpersonal relationships, challenging situations and general stress.

If you are going through difficult times, in relationships or otherwise, this may be the "mental cleansing" you need to see you through. Done daily or even several times a day, it will extricate your attention from your problems or pain.

If you think back to a period in your life when you were very upset, you will recognize that you weren't as aware of your surroundings as you usually are. Sights and colors were dull. You couldn't think clearly or come up with solutions to problems. You weren't as productive, and your judgment was poor.

This exercise, done correctly and sufficiently, can lift anyone out of the fog of unhappiness and into the brightness of regained clarity.

EXERCISE

Go out and take a walk. It doesn't matter what time of day or for how long. It doesn't matter how fast you walk—this isn't a workout. Walk around and look at your surroundings: the streets, cars, buildings, homes, trees, gardens....

You will find that at first you are still preoccupied with your problems. That's normal. Keep walking and *force* yourself to notice your surroundings. Keep doing so until you feel better.

Don't take your phone with you and spend your walking time talking to someone. You will defeat the purpose of this exercise, which is to pull your attention *away* from your upset to your present surroundings and bring you from "then" to "now."

If you've received bad news, had an argument or a disturbing phone conversation, don't lock yourself up in your room or sit in front of the TV. Instead take a walk and look around.

If you have a tough decision to make, don't make it while you're worried or upset. Upset people make bad decisions. Take daily walks—for weeks, if you must—until you feel better. You will find that you have regained your clarity, and can now trust yourself to make the right decisions to elevate your life.

This exercise can be done anytime and as often as you wish: in the morning before going to work, during your lunch break or before going to bed. (You will, of course, make sure that the neighborhood you walk through is safe.) It is refreshing after being in front of the computer or working indoors for hours.

It is sometimes necessary to do this exercise before doing Exercise 7, "Recognizing Red Flags," as your clarity of mind will help you be more objective.

CHAPTER 9

*T*HE TOXIC MATE: WHEN TO RUN THE OTHER WAY

CHAPTER 9

*T*HE TOXIC MATE: WHEN TO RUN THE OTHER WAY

You may have heard that some people are "toxic." You get them into your life and, sooner or later, you start going downhill. They may be hard to detect. Like fighting with a shadow, they make it difficult to pinpoint what's wrong. They can be so nice at times, and you may enjoy their company. Yet, if you look back, you may discover that you started doing worse right around the time they appeared in your life.

If you've ever had a relationship with a Toxic Mate, you undoubtedly have scars to show and horror stories to tell. But what exactly is a *toxic mate*? How can you recognize him/her, and what can you do if you fall for one?

The skill of identifying Toxic Personalities is vital not only to Picking Right. A relative or a friend (or rather "friend," because they are worse than any enemy you might have) could also be a Toxic Personality. As such, they don't help your existence. Instead, they do you in: openly and obviously, or secretly behind the scenes. They are a minority (most people are good and mean well), but it takes only one Toxic Personality to ruin a life.

Your best weapon is the knowledge to detect them. And once you do, get them out of your life without sorrow or regret.

TWO FACES

You can expect the Toxic Mate to be two-faced. He or she creates false impressions and gives false hopes while doing something else behind your back. The person may even be leading a whole other life that you know nothing of.

I am reminded of a girl who was barely twenty years old when she started dating a charming man. She loved their excursions out of town, dining by the ocean and engaging in intellectual conversations. They found so much in common!

After a few weeks of dating he disappeared. Puzzled and distressed, she spoke to a girlfriend who suggested that she go to his hometown and find out what happened to him.

She mustered up her courage and got on the road. She didn't have an address, only the name of the small community where he supposedly lived.

When she got there, she asked a passerby about her man. "He lives over there," he pointed. "I don't think he is home now, but his wife is...."

The man she fell for was a Toxic Mate. He was two-faced and led double, triple or multiple lives. He wasn't worth pursuing. He existed in the shadows of his own deception. One might feel sorry for his wife and then move on, never to look back.

PLAYING THE FIELD

The Player—the guy or gal who dates several people at once— is a Toxic Mate. If you are in search of a long-lasting relationship and the other person wants to play the field, realize that your goals don't match. Don't *waste* yourself on a Player.

Samantha said this about the man who broke her heart: "I was hoping he'd had a change of heart, but probably not. He could change if he wanted to, but he is comfortable with his life the way it is. I remember him saying, 'Why change if you like what you have?'"

Precisely! You like your car. It gets you where you want to go. It projects the image you wish to project. Why change? That's the Player's mentality. And so, most people who make reforming a Player their life's project gain nothing but heartache.

It is true that people *can* and *do* change, but don't hold your breath or waste your best years waiting. Realize that a Player has used up and spit out many people's beauty, love and devotion. Chances are they will do the same to yours.

And even if they do reform, they aren't likely to bring into their new life people who were "notches on their belt" in their past life. When they put the past behind them, they also leave behind the people in it.

So don't be a notch on someone's belt. There is no shortage of people, and you *can* find happiness with someone who values you and all you can give in a relationship.

> ### "You may delay, but time will not."
> —Benjamin Franklin

NONCOMMITTAL

If you are in search of the Right Pick, you are also seeking commitment. You wish to build a relationship that will lead to long-lasting happiness. Obviously, you don't expect anyone to make a premature commitment to you, nor will you commit yourself to them before you get to know them. But be aware of their intentions, so you know whether or not they are a worthy candidate.

The following real-life example may not be easy to follow, but in the interest of Picking Right, it should be.

Heather was a beautiful divorcee who enjoyed the company and courtship of a wealthy charmer. A lifelong bachelor, Eric was intrigued by the fact that she refused to get intimate with him unless he committed.

"I have zero interest in a one-night stand," she said, "If you aren't interested in a serious relationship, let's just be friends." And friends, she implied, don't come with "benefits."

Heather realized that a noncommittal partner would be a Toxic Mate to her. She'd be wasting her time and breaking her heart longing for that commitment. Rather than being an equal partner, she'd have an inferior position in the relationship, being the one to beg and wish that Eric would love her the way she deserved to be loved.

Women are not the only ones to experience this. Men do too. Male or female, this is a toxic situation that makes life miserable and is harmful to one's self-respect and self-worth.

If you appreciate yourself, run the other way!

WEIRD STUFF

People who are involved in extracurricular sexual activities could be Toxic Mates. If your mate is into pornography, strip clubs, orgies, kinky or perverted sexual practices, beware. That is, if you are fairly straightforward yourself.

This is not a lesson in morality. Experience will show you that there are deeper issues behind such activities. Look and you will find them.

Moreover, since such conduct is not socially accepted, these people are usually forced to hide their activities. This gets them into a deceitful state of mind and establishes dishonest practices. And any dishonest mate is a Toxic Mate to you.

THE WAY OUT

Almost anyone who has Picked Wrong (and who hasn't?) will tell you that they noticed the red flags early on but refused to accept them for what they were. That was the case in this next real-life story.

During their first months of dating, Evelyn believed that she had met the man of her dreams. Never before had she had a relationship so smooth and simple. Then trouble began. Keith regularly accused her of flirting with waiters in restaurants and of sleeping with every man she talked to. She even started doubting herself: Could it be he was right for criticizing her?

The truth is, Keith was psychotic. He kept guns in the trunk of his car and had an evil mother running his life. His accusations were the red flags Evelyn refused to see.

Finally she came to her senses. She left town in a hurry, escaping the relationship and probably saving her own life.

The Toxic Mate *can* be identified early on. The red flags *are* there. The relationship is a confusing mixture of good and bad that keeps you hoping. That hope and confusion are the glue that sticks you to your mate.

The answer is to be brutally honest about it—there is no substitute for that. It will hurt, but not as much as ruining your life will.

Exercise 8, "Gaining Clarity," will help you deal with this successfully.

Additionally, do this: Distance yourself from your problem for a moment and pretend that you are giving advice to a friend who has your situation. What do you think about the red flags in that relationship? And how would you advise your friend?

Most probably, that's the advice you yourself should take.

EXERCISE 9
Identifying the Toxic Mate

Note: It is recommended that you fill in your answers on a
separate sheet of paper or make a copy of these pages.

If you have ever had a relationship with a Toxic Mate, you can
probably recognize in him/her some of the traits mentioned here.

Even if you have been fortunate enough to escape such a
relationship, you probably know someone who wasn't as lucky, and
so you've come to know a Toxic Mate through somebody else's story.

The purpose of this exercise is to sharpen your skills in recognizing
a Toxic Mate and so lessen the chance that you would ever fall prey
to one.

EXAMPLE

Think back to one such Toxic Mate—yours or someone else's. Now
recall specific times when this person manifested his or her "toxic"
nature as described in this chapter.

Can you recall a relationship where someone was *Two-Faced?*

_____

_____

_____

Can you recall a relationship where someone was *Playing the Field?*

_____

_____

_____

Can you recall a relationship where someone was *Noncommittal*?

_____

_____

_____

Can you recall a relationship where someone was into *Weird Stuff*?

_____

_____

_____

HOW TO MAKE A FRESH START

HOW TO MAKE A FRESH START

Now that we've covered the pitfalls of Picking Right, let's look to the future. Let's see what you'll need to do to make a fresh start and be well on your way to finding your match.

If you have a history of Picking Wrong, this is an important chapter for you. It will empower you to put bad choices behind you and enable you to Pick Right.

One or more of the following scenarios might describe you:

- You want to know how to Pick Right.
- You keep choosing the same wrong personality type, relationship after relationship.
- You are unable to let go of a Toxic Mate or a destructive relationship.
- You and your partner know you are wrong for each other but you can't let go.

WHAT'S WRONG WITH BEING WRONG?

When a relationship fails, it leaves its mark. If we choose to end it, we may feel wrong for having started it. If our mate breaks it off, we may feel even worse. Failures pile up throughout a lifetime, making us feel wrong in our choices or actions.

No one likes to be wrong. Seeking to be right is human nature. The truth of the matter is you are always right. Because at any point in your life, you made the right choice based on the information you had.

As in purchasing a car or a home, your decisions are based on what you know or are able to find out. Sometimes the car has engine problems, or the house plumbing issues, that aren't easily discoverable. One's decisions are always right, based on the information at hand, as the following real-life story illustrates.

Lorrie had moved from Alaska to California, where she met Ken. Ken had a good job, and they got along well. Their future together looked promising, so they decided to move in together and invite Lorrie's mother to join them. They were planning to rent a house together to keep expenses down.

All went well until an alert landlord did a routine background check as part of a rental application. Ken had several instances of domestic violence and a few DUIs on his record. When the landlord shared the information with Lorrie and her mother, they were shocked. They hadn't suspected any of it! And the fact that Ken had hidden his past from them further put his honesty in question. The relationship ended promptly.

Picking Right can be challenging. We do our best to judge correctly, but we don't always know that we don't know. To make matters worse, we've been told that we "shouldn't judge."

Shouldn't judge! You are about to join your heart and life with another human being and you haven't the right to judge? Whose life is it anyway? And who is going to suffer the consequences of a bad choice?

You *must* regard your prospective mate with a critical eye. Look for red flags and have a probation period, as discussed in an earlier chapter. Now is the time to judge, and the purpose of this book is to provide you effective tools to judge correctly so that you may Pick Right.

BREAKING UP IS HARD TO DO

Supposing you fell for someone's charm and (initial) good behavior; then not until later did the truth come out, and you discovered the detrimental effect this person could have on your life. Still, breaking up would be painful.

The following real-life story illustrates that.

Dave called a drug-abuse hotline for advice. He wanted to know how to help his girlfriend, who, he said, was using "some drugs."

She would disappear for days, she didn't work, and she lived off him. Being a decent and sober man, he didn't understand life under the influence.

Substance abusers have one thing in mind: their next fix. They use and abuse people in their life in order to get it, and they give little or nothing in return.

This doesn't mean they are bad people. It is the nature of addiction to take over the person's life and rob them of honor and dignity. Contrary to some beliefs, addiction is not an incurable disease. It is a terrible condition for which there is only one solution: sobriety. And sobriety *can* be attained.

Dave loved the girl and wanted to help her. But she was the wrong girl to love. The only help she needed was effective drug treatment. Although he was miserable in the relationship, he refused to face reality.

We could consider Dave naive or stupid, but he was neither. He had Picked Wrong, and he stayed in the relationship in an effort to

109

prove that he was right. Breaking up with his girlfriend would be an admission of wrongness, and that goes against human nature.

BREAKING A VICIOUS CYCLE

What can you do if you fall for the wrong person? In spite of unhappiness, drama and abuse, you can't let go. Perhaps you've even broken up but, deep inside, you haven't moved on. Stuck on the wrong person, you of course ruin your chances of Picking Right.

Knowing what you now know about the human urge to be right, you can help yourself overcome it (if it stands in the way of your happiness) and move on to build a better life. For the glue that keeps you stuck in a bad relationship is the refusal to admit that you've Picked Wrong and the desire—even *obsession*—to be right.

WHAT TO DO

Let's consider your troublesome relationship. Obviously, you have good reasons to like this individual. So ask yourself: *What do I love about them? What do I like about the relationship?* Consider their wonderful qualities and all the good they bring into your life.

Undoubtedly you tried to tell this to your friends or family, but they contradicted you. Perhaps they even told you to open your eyes and stop being an idiot. They didn't realize that your natural reaction to such contradiction would be to assert yourself and insist that you are right to love the person who is causing you so much grief. Instead of criticizing, they should have heard you out. They didn't, and that didn't help.

The following real-life story illustrates what could have happened had someone listened correctly.

Christina had a boyfriend who had little going for him. He seldom worked, nor did he go to school. He didn't treat her particularly well, at least not consistently. And he had no ambition to get anywhere in life. Naturally, her family disapproved of the relationship and expressed their disapproval openly. When that proved useless, she could still see the frustration in their eyes. People's emotions and opinions are often felt whether or not they express them in words.

One day Christina came to my office having had an argument with her boyfriend. I asked her to tell me what she liked about him and about their relationship. Without offering advice or opinion, I listened attentively and let her know that I understood. I really did understand.

This was the first time Christina could talk about her relationship without being judged or told that she was wrong. I left it at that.

Next time I saw Christina she mentioned that she had broken up with her boyfriend. She was relieved and felt that she had made the right decision. She was ready to get on with her life and find a better match.

Human beings seek to be right. When they are constantly contradicted, as was Christina, they hold on to their erroneous views, bad habits and miserable relationships, just to "be right." On the other hand, if they are allowed to express their views without judgment, they may change their minds.

Talking freely about something can be extremely therapeutic. No wonder we refer to it as "bouncing something off" someone. As we bring the matter out of our inner world and describe it to another person, we see things we couldn't see before and so gain clarity.

But this only happens if we feel safe to express ourselves without the risk of being analyzed, criticized or judged.

Often, people wish to help us by correcting us or showing us how wrong we are. Isn't that what our parents, teachers, friends and others have done? Was it helpful? No. We needed someone who would lend an ear, so that we might see the light for ourselves.

This principle can also be applied to any habit, such as smoking or overeating. Just ask the person what they like about it, and let them tell you why it is right that they do what they do. Don't analyze or criticize; don't agree or disagree. Just listen and let them know that they've been heard and understood. You might help them get unstuck from an old, destructive habit.

DO IT YOURSELF

Since you may not find someone who will calmly listen to your excuses about picking an abusive mate or staying in a miserable relationship, you might have to do it yourself.

The thing to do is make a list (call it an "inventory") of everything you love about the person (with whom you are miserable) and the (rotten/destructive/awful) relationship you have with him or her. Write it all out and satisfy yourself that you have covered all the good present in it. Then set the list aside or shred it, as you please. (See the next exercise for complete instructions.)

Some days or weeks later you might find that the "glue" sticking you to this person and to the relationship is wearing off, and that you are finally able to think clearly and make a decision about it: either fix it to your full satisfaction or end it for good!

EXERCISE 10
The Inventory

Note: It is recommended that you fill in your answers on a
separate sheet of paper or make a copy of the next page.

The Inventory can be used to help you get over a bad relationship you
are still stuck on. You can also use it to help a friend or a loved one
who needs to extract themselves from an abusive relationship. Do
your own inventory and/or have them do theirs.

A WORD OF CAUTION

In helping another do their inventory, never offer your opinion or
advice regarding anything they say. Do not agree or disagree with
them. And do not analyze, criticize or pass judgment, no matter how
foolish they may sound.

It is vital that you make them feel safe to express themselves fully.
They don't need your input. Their relationship is a trap of sorts. It
is confusing, and no amount of words will unconfuse it for them.
Trapped in it, they cannot see what's in front of them.

Like a person who would break out of a prison, they need to be
able to *look* at the walls and fences, gates and locks before they can
see the way out. If you do this right, they will recognize that the walls
don't really exist and that the gate is wide open, waiting for them to
step out to a better life.

Be aware, though, that such realization might not happen right
before your eyes. So let them answer your questions until they run
out of answers. Some days or weeks may pass before you realize that
you have helped them successfully.

113

HELPING YOURSELF

In doing this exercise yourself, write down the answers to the following questions. If a few days from now you come up with additional information, add it to your inventory. Then set it aside.

1. What do you like about him/her?

_____

_____

_____

_____

2. What do you like about your relationship with him/her?

_____

_____

_____

_____

_____

HELPING ANOTHER

Ask the person the above questions. Acknowledge their answers, letting them know that you understand what they say. That's all.

Some days or weeks later you, or the person you are trying to help, might find that your (or their) outlook has changed, and that you (or they) are now able to make decisions that will lead to greater happiness and to Picking Right.

CHAPTER 11

*A*RE YOU READY FOR YOUR MATCH?

ARE YOU READY FOR YOUR MATCH?

When the right match comes along, you want to be ready. Preparing yourself for the right person takes more than "putting the past behind you" or "thinking positive thoughts" with the hope of attracting nothing but good. It may require that you yourself change in order to be worthy of the quality person you want in your life.

In the past, perhaps you settled for players, cheaters and noncommittal relationships. And maybe that was fine while you were out to "have a good time" and test your powers as a woman or a man. But if you are reading this book, I assume you've "been there, done that" and you are now ready for real love that lasts a lifetime.

WHAT ARE YOU LOOKING FOR?

Do you know what you want in a lifelong mate? What are the important qualities that form a sound foundation for a fulfilling relationship, and one that has lasting power? Remember, we assume that you have been through the fly-by-nighters and are ready for the real thing.

Looks aren't it. No matter how gorgeous he or she may be now, the person will not look this way in thirty or forty years; but neither will you. Sad but true: physical beauty is impermanent. Fortunately, beauty is both internal and external. You have undoubtedly met someone who was good looking, until they opened their mouth. If we care about inner beauty as much as outer beauty—well, that does not wear out with age. Furthermore, as your bond deepens, your mate can be beautiful to you in ways no one else may comprehend.

Whatever you decide regarding looks, when it comes to fidelity and overall honesty, there is no compromise. Most relationships come to ruin on the rock of deception. Couples may stay together for kids or money, but their love seldom recovers from the blow of dishonesty. Even if the truth remains hidden or unspoken, the accumulated secrets erect a wall between them that destroys their happiness. So, as covered earlier, honesty is indispensable.

As you will see in a later chapter, there are specific compatibility points that are key to the long-term success of your relationship.

Additionally, you want someone who will reciprocate: give back the love, help, consideration and hard work that you are willing to invest; someone who will appreciate you for who you are and for all you do for your union.

There may be other qualities.

That said, it's time for you to get ready. But how?

DO YOU SETTLE FOR LESS?

Have you ever known someone who settled for less than they deserved? Have you ever done so? This is a sure way to Pick Wrong, as did Betty.

She was frustrated: "Why can't I find my match?" For years, she had been in and out of relationships—some longer than others, but all of them troublesome, and none lasted. She was beautiful, intelligent, loyal and kind. She deserved better. Her "fate" was a puzzle to her, but not to me.

118

Betty had a knack for picking selfish, borderline-abusive men. They certainly did not provide the care and appreciation she hoped to get from a mate, and which she willingly provided in her relationships. She needed to raise her own standards!

If you settle for less, you will get less. In the world of employment, you know your worth and you go in expecting a certain pay. You don't settle for less than your expertise, experience and education call for. Yet, when it comes to relationships, many fine men and women lower their standards and settle for less than they deserve.

The pay of a relationship is the love, understanding and support that help both of you lead a better life. A relationship that brings grief, that makes you feel unimportant, less valuable, less attractive, is a drain. It isn't worth having.

So your first step in getting ready for your Right Pick is to raise your standards. Raise them to suit what you deserve.

Of course, some people will tell you that you are not realistic. Don't listen to them. They are talking out of their own disappointments and low standards. If you put your mind to it and work hard at it, almost anything is possible—perhaps anything is.

Fortunately, unlike a job, being without a relationship for a while will not devastate you. You will not starve or get evicted. You are better off keeping clear of those substandard relationships and investing your energy and time in the search for the Right Pick than accumulating scars and wasting years of your life.

Some people can't stand the "vacuum" of no relationship. They have to have someone in their life all the time. However, finding the Right Pick may require that you tolerate being on your own for a while. Without a "vacancy" in your life, he or she may pass you by. If you wish to fill the "seat" next to you with that special person, keep it empty. Don't occupy it with a substitute and expect things to magically work out when Mr. or Miss Perfect appears on the scene.

"It is better to be alone
than in bad company."
—George Washington

ARE YOU WORTHY?

Whatever you demand of your mate, be sure that you can deliver in kind. Are you generous? Are you trustworthy? Are you willing to work hard to preserve the relationship and care for him or her?

Although wedding ceremonies declare that it's "through thick and thin," are you truly ready for the "thin" side of life? Are you prepared to be there for your mate when he or she looks pale in a hospital bed or when he or she isn't much fun after a hard day of work? Are you willing to give as much as you receive, and more?

Simply put, are you ready to be a *good friend* to your mate—his or her *best* friend?

A good relationship, and one that has longevity, is a friendship. It is a spiritual bond, really, between two people. Yes, it includes sexual activity and economic aspects, and there may be other people involved, such as children and extended family. But at its core, it is a *spiritual* bond. If you have ever known an old couple, where the surviving spouse didn't last long after the other had passed, you know that it's true.

As covered earlier, a relationship, like any true friendship, must be clear of deception. This doesn't mean we never do anything wrong—we aren't angels. It means that we do all we can to do what's right and to be honest.

120

This is a tall order, especially considering the way we've been raised and what we may have witnessed. However, the growing divorce rate clearly demonstrates that change is in order.

Perhaps we can set a better example for others, even establish new standards. Perhaps we can create a whole new relationship culture, where couples are happy and families stay together.

> *"True friendship is*
> *a plant of slow growth,*
> *and must undergo and withstand*
> *the shocks of adversity before*
> *it is entitled to the appellation."* *
> —George Washington

MOVING ON

There are no angels on Earth. There is no person alive who hasn't done something they aren't proud of or are afraid will be found out. So join the crowd. This doesn't mean people are bad. It means we aren't perfect. Fortunately the past is not as important as the future, and the future is ahead of us.

Even a criminal could change his or her ways and become an asset to society far in excess of any damage done. Similarly, a formerly "bad partner" could become an ideal spouse if he or she chooses to. We create our lives every waking hour. And we can change our future with every new decision and action. The choice is ours!

Aaron was a good example of this.

He cheated on every girlfriend he had and felt no remorse. On the contrary, while living a life of women and booze, he truly believed himself to be a good catch and a great mate.

---

*appellation: name or title.   121

People can change, and so did he, but not without a brave and honest look in the mirror.

Following some spiritual work and a written inventory of his wild escapades, Aaron had the blinding realization that he'd been a dreadful mate in all his relationships. He decided to change and, for the first time in his life, created a monogamous relationship that promises to be long lasting.

THE STORY OF ONE BRAVE WOMAN

The following testimonial illustrates how one woman applied herself to put a painful past behind her and prepare for a better future.

"Many years ago I experienced a bad relationship breakup that left me in shock and pain. There was nothing I could do about it. I was heartbroken and felt helpless. I detested being at the mercy of another who had betrayed me. I knew it was up to me to pick myself back up and take control of my life. I needed to put the past behind me and turn a new leaf.

"I decided that, rather than dwell on my misery, I should review the harm I had caused others in my previous relationships. I hadn't killed anyone but, like most human beings, I had mistreated good people and had done things I wasn't proud of. Many times I broke the Golden Rule by failing to treat others the way I wanted to be treated, or by doing to them what I didn't want done to me.

"I started writing. I wrote pages upon pages of long-forgotten misdeeds. The more I wrote, the more I remembered. As my memory improved, my 'inventory' expanded beyond relationships and embraced other parts of life: family, school, work, friendships. I was purging my inner self, sweeping things out from under the rug and cleaning house. This spiritual spring cleaning took courage. It wasn't easy. But it changed my life forever.

"When I was done writing, I knew I was done. I was relieved. I felt light and happy. A big weight had lifted off me—weight I didn't even know was there until it was gone.

"To my amazement, I was no longer heartbroken. My upset over the recent breakup had vanished! I couldn't even feel anger toward my ex for what he had done to me. Could this be the result of the work I had just done in reviewing, not what had been done to me, but what I had done to others?

"At last I am guilt-free. I am ready and able to turn a new leaf. I know I deserve to find the man of my dreams and have the happy, loving relationship I've always longed for."

THE CONFESSION

What our brave woman did could be called a *Self-Imposed Confession*, an *Inventory* or a *Do-It-Yourself Spiritual Cleanse*. Whatever you call it, it is a hard look in the mirror and a brave look at one's actions. It is a responsible look at what one may have done to bring about one's "fate."

As mentioned in an earlier chapter, *responsibility* is not *fault, guilt* or *blame*. Rather, it is the willingness to admit that—through one's decisions, choices and actions—one had a hand in bringing about one's present condition.

You must be a "big person" to be *responsible*. And being so could take your relationship, and indeed your entire life, to a whole new level.

If you are going to do your Self-Confession, it is a good idea to shred your notes when you are done. Someone else might not appreciate your high responsibility level and try to use it against you. Since the benefit is in the writing, not the record keeping, once you are done, your notes are no longer needed.

Contrary to popular belief, we aren't as much disturbed by the times we were mistreated by others as by the times we mistreated them. Good people seldom forgive themselves and may carry deep and forgotten guilt for years to come. Facing our own misdeeds is liberating and can be a significant step in preparing us for our match and for the happy relationship we've been longing for.

The following exercise has changed many lives for the better. It is well worth doing.

"When I do good, I feel good.
When I do bad, I feel bad.
That's my religion."
—Abraham Lincoln

EXERCISE 11
Your Self-Confession

Use separate sheets of paper for this exercise. When you are done, shred them. You don't need them for your records. They are perfectly recorded—in your mind. This is your private cleanse. Leaving your notes around opens the door for some faultfinding personality to discover them and throw your misdeeds in your face. By doing this exercise you are already making a change and taking responsibility for your actions. That's to be commended!

EXERCISE

Ask yourself:

- What have I done that I am not proud of?
- What have I done that I regret?
- What have I done that I've had to hide from others?

Write your answers with all details. While you focus on relationships, should some misdeeds come to mind that involve your family, friends or work, write them down too. They surface because you have attention on them or have felt guilty about them at some point in time. You might as well get them off your chest while you are at it.

Ask yourself these additional questions:

- In relationships, who am I most upset about?
- Who broke my heart worse than anyone else?
- Who do I feel deepest resentment toward?

This may sound strange, but now ask yourself this:

- What have I done to this person?
- What secrets have I kept from him/her?

And write down everything you can remember.

It may sound unlikely that you should expect relief from putting down what you have done to someone who has wronged you. But what is there to lose? You haven't experienced relief dwelling on what they've done to you. So cleanse your side of the coin, until it shines!

If this exercise made you feel better, write me. I am very interested!

A WORD OF CAUTION

At first this exercise will make you feel worse. That's not the time to stop. Keep writing. Once your self-confession is complete, you will feel much better. You will be relieved and happier.

But don't let that make you forget to shred your notes.

"Confession of errors
is like a broom
which sweeps away the dirt
and leaves the surface
brighter and clearer."
—Mahatma Gandhi

CHAPTER 12

THREE VITAL RULES FOR PICKING RIGHT

CHAPTER 12

*T*HREE VITAL RULES FOR PICKING RIGHT

The following *Vital Rules for Picking Right* are worth their weight in gold. If you inspect your own relationships or those of people around you, you will see that the mysteries of compatibility are solved with these three rules.

Read on. Examine some relationships, and see if this is true for you.

THE RACEHORSE AND THE MULE

Some people say that opposites attract. Perhaps they do. Be that as it may, the important question is, does "being opposites" make for a happy relationship?

Young Mike and Marlene were "opposites" and they were in love. Mike was active and energetic. He was quick to make decisions and act on them. He was always on the go and got a lot done—fast! Marlene, on the other hand, "traveled" at a much slower pace. She could watch TV for hours and take all day to prepare a meal that he could whip up in no time at all.

They got married and…drove each other crazy! To her, he was "impatient." To him, she was "lazy." The relationship was frustrating to both of them.

Why? Their speed. Imagine doing a project with a coworker whose speed is very different from yours—faster or slower. One of you wants to get the letters in the mail immediately, while the other is still contemplating what to write. Here are a "racehorse" and a "mule" pulling a cart together, and both are frustrated.

I am reminded of a walk I once took in these magnificent gardens with a friend. She was overweight and suffered from asthma. The poor woman tired easily and had to stop frequently to rest. She felt bad for me, and I felt sorry for her. Neither one of us enjoyed the walk.

So ask yourself: *How fast do I "travel" in life? How quickly do I get things done? How long do I take to make a decision? And once decided, how long before I act on it?*

Now, compare yourself to your partner. Are you similar speedwise or is one of you much faster than the other? If your speed is comparable, you will have an easier time getting along. If it isn't, you will find it difficult to coexist.

In pulling life's cart, a Right Pick is a partner who is similar to you, whichever you are, a racehorse or a mule. When it comes to speed, pick your match, not your opposite.

VITAL RULE #1
Similar Speed is key to a successful relationship.
When it comes to speed, pick your match, not your opposite.

EMOTIONS

One's attitude toward life, how they *feel* about it, the kind of emotions they experience and display, varies from person to person. Some people are cheerful and optimistic in their approach, while others respond to life's challenges with anger, worry or despair.

You may recall the anticipation and excitement of your first day at school. (Where did it go, by the way?) Enthusiasm is a young child's attitude toward life. By the time he is in college, he might experience anxiety. By his golden years, he is not so "golden" anymore: sadness and apathy may have set in.

As life hammers us with challenges, disappointments, failures, losses, illness, shocks, accidents—you name it—negative emotions set in. We may become resentful. We worry. We have regrets. We may feel sad about the past and anxious about the future. Life is no longer as bright, and the future is not as promising.

Some people manage to stay interested and excited in spite of all. We consider them "dynamic." Perhaps their burden is not as great. Perhaps they are just tougher than most. Be it as it may, they remain driven and excited about life. Yet others, having experienced one too many failures, lower their expectations or even give up their hopes. They become sad, reserved, cautious. The pain life dishes out—both emotional and physical—would do that to a person, and down he or she goes.

Having a comparable emotional approach to life is vital to a successful relationship.

MISMATCH

Have you ever known an upbeat person whose mate was at the other end of the spectrum: sad, depressed and pessimistic about life? Perhaps this person even tried to help their mate, but the outcome was poor.

Like the racehorse and the mule, this is a mismatch. The upbeat partner tries to uplift the other and inject him/her with excitement and hope. He or she tries in vain to convince the other that life is worthwhile, that it can be good in spite of all, and that the future is what you make it.

You should know that the upbeat partner always loses, because they get drained of their life energy through their efforts to bring the other up.

Have you ever tried to cheer up a grieving person or uplift someone who was going through a breakup? Did your words of wisdom fall on deaf ears? Exactly! Because you spoke from a place of hope, while this person "knew" there was none. And by the end of it, you were drained.

Now imagine going through this with your life partner on a daily basis!

Suppose a man loses his job. Now he worries about losing the house and everything he has worked for. He feels like a failure and that he has let his family down.

His wife gives him a cheer-up speech about updating his résumé and sending it to all corners of the globe; perhaps taking this opportunity to retrain for a better-paying position or to start the business he has always dreamed of. To her, the future can be bright because it is what you make it. It is a blank canvas on which they can paint their destiny. This may be a blessing in disguise!

To him, the past is a disappointment and the future is a jungle filled with threats. So he collects unemployment and watches a lot of TV to "help" himself cope with the stress, while she gets more and more frustrated with each passing day.

Some people believe that finance is the most common cause for divorce. When it is, it is only the surface reason, and a careful inspection will reveal the true causes. One key reason is a discrepancy in the partners' emotional approach toward life, as described here. Such difference results in different attitudes toward finance and financial stress.

When one partner approaches life with hope and energy while the other is too bored to be concerned about success or too afraid to try; if one attacks problems with determination while the other gives up without a fight, trouble is guaranteed.

BUT WHAT ABOUT HELPING?

Dynamic people may overlook the emotional differences between them and their mates because of a desire to help, as did these women.

Sharon was obsessed with an unloving mate because she found in him someone she could help. She married him and put up with tremendous abuse, including low productivity, lack of affection and even extramarital affairs.

* * *

Jody felt sympathy for her husband, a compassion for his rough upbringing and a compulsion to help or "save" him. Consequently, she tolerated low productivity and an unbalanced relationship. Not only did she work and earn most of the income but she also carried the burden of the household chores and responsibilities.

Beware of sympathy! Never start a relationship with someone for whom you feel sorry. It is a recipe for disaster.

Of course, you *want* to help. Your desire to help is a mark of your goodness. Furthermore, help is a vital part of life. A newborn baby wouldn't last a day without help, and none of us would be alive today without it. If not for such help, I wouldn't be here writing this book, and you wouldn't be there reading it. We've all received help, and we all must give it.

However, a relationship where the scales are grossly unbalanced, where help is one sided, where one partner is the savior and giver while the other is the taker, is unhealthy and will not last—at least not happily. Your mate should be of similar powers and needs as you, so that the give-and-take is comparable.

Some people arouse sympathy in us. As good people, we see their potential and wish to help. While that is honorable, do it at your own risk. This mushy emotion called "sympathy" is an unhealthy ingredient in a relationship. Use it to save a dying person or rescue an animal, but please don't marry someone for whom you feel sorry!

MUTUAL EMPOWERMENT

The Right Pick is a person whose attitude and approach to life are similar to yours—someone who has a comparable level of excitement, drive and ambition. If your mate is much more intense than you, the relationship will be stressful for you and frustrating for them. And vice versa.

Imagine *Mr. Go-Getter* going home each night to *Mrs. Down* and trying to lift her from her boredom or hopelessness.

Or *Mrs. Motivation* going home to *Mr. Negativity* and trying to inject life into him.

The ideal scenario is *Mr. Go-Getter* plus *Mrs. Motivation*! Here you have a couple that energize each other. They bring their individual strengths and happiness into the relationship, and neither one gets drained. They will go far in life too.

In Picking Right, don't go after a mate you must continually prop up. Find someone whose emotional approach to life is comparable to yours. Life is sure to present you with challenges, so leave the one-sided propping for those special circumstances. As long as you are similar in your emotional attitudes toward life, you will spend most of your lives empowering one another.

VITAL RULE #2

A Similar Emotional Approach to life is vital to a successful relationship. Pick a mate who has a comparable emotional attitude to yours, and you'll empower each other.

WHAT DO YOU WANT OUT OF LIFE?

Most couples suffer from short-term thinking.

When love is young and new, the focus is on the little things they find in common: the type of food they like, their taste in music or art, and their love for dance or the outdoors. Besides, sex is good, and they make a cute couple.

Although being compatible on these levels is nice, it is not necessarily the mark of a good match, for these are superficial issues. Let's look deeper: let's consider goals. What does each of you want out of life?

Suppose a man in his forties is ready to settle down and raise a family. The woman he loves has a thriving career as a dancer, which she refuses to disrupt with pregnancy for the next decade, if ever. They are happy together and go on dating for several years.

Sooner or later they'll be forced to face the fact that their goals don't match. They don't have the same destination in mind. How could they travel life's journey together?

A couple's goals are like the instruments of an orchestra. They must be in harmony with one another. While they need not be identical, they must not clash but must be achievable side by side.

A politician married a woman who regarded public service as an uncalled-for sacrifice of family life.

135

When they met, he'd been in politics for two decades. His career was an inseparable part of his life. Clearly, it was important to him.

A woman who resents sacrificing her life to public service has no business marrying a politician!

There can be other goal-related discrepancies.

One woman was very much into personal development. To her, life's spiritual side was senior to building wealth, living comfortably or working toward retirement. Her fiancé, on the other hand, was a down-to-earth businessman who considered spiritual pursuits a waste of time. Both overlooked their differences, each secretly hoping that the other would move over to their side of the tracks.

After two years of tiptoeing around each other, they finally dared discuss the matter. She quickly learned that he opposed her spiritual pursuits and intended to restrict them as soon as they were married. Obviously he didn't know the woman he was with because, to his amazement, she promptly started packing to leave.

So goals are a significant factor in a relationship. They must not clash but be achievable side by side.

Don't waste precious time hoping. Put the cards on the table and discuss your respective goals early in the relationship. If you find discrepancies, don't bury your head in the sand. Sooner or later they will come back to haunt you. So try to settle your differences now. Find solutions that will permit each of you to attain your respective goals. Your happiness depends on it.

And face it: if you absolutely cannot align your goals, you don't belong together.

One final note about goals: they may need to be updated periodically. People grow and change, and their aspirations change with them. Whereas they didn't want kids when they first met, now they do. Where previously they had wanted kids early in life, now they want to have a career first. So regardless of your initial agreements, things can change and new agreements may need to be established.

Your best tool is communication. Keep it open and sincere, and permit each other to communicate anything and everything. You will then know about any new goals or change of goals, and you can align yourselves to each other newly.

VITAL RULE #3
Matching Goals are essential to a successful relationship.
Make sure your goals do not clash, but harmonize.

THE THREE VITAL RULES

VITAL RULE #1
Similar Speed is key to a successful relationship.
When it comes to speed, pick your match, not your opposite.

VITAL RULE #2
A Similar Emotional Approach to life is vital to a successful
relationship. Pick a mate who has a comparable emotional
attitude to yours, and you'll empower each other.

VITAL RULE #3
Matching Goals are essential to a successful relationship.
Make sure your goals do not clash, but harmonize.

EXERCISE 12
The Three Vital Rules: Predicting the Future of Your Relationship

Note: It is recommended that you fill in your answers on a
separate sheet of paper or make a copy of this page.

You can assess and grade any relationship using the *Three Vital Rules for Picking Right*. A couple may have different tastes in music or food, even different religious beliefs or cultural backgrounds, and still have what it takes to create a happy union. But if their discrepancies lie within the *Three Vital Rules*, they don't stand a chance.

Fortunately, if you and your mate are a near match, this assessment will pinpoint what you could work on in order to create even greater harmony. If you share this exercise with him/her and work as a team to improve your situation, you should expect stellar results.

	Mostly	Sometimes	No/Seldom
We function at a similar speed in life	___	___	___
Our emotional attitude/approach toward life is similar	___	___	___
Our goals match/harmonize	___	___	___

If you got all "Mostly," your relationship has a great potential. Keep up the good work, and keep the harmony going.

If you got all "No/Seldom," you have a lot of work ahead of you. But at least you know the root of your trouble now and what must change.

Any other combination of answers gives you an idea of the amount of work needed to create a truly happy, long-lasting relationship.

CHAPTER 13

*Y*OUR RELATIONSHIP CHECKLIST

CHAPTER 13

YOUR RELATIONSHIP CHECKLIST

People rarely get into a car and drive away without a destination in mind. Yet they regularly get into relationships without deciding where they want them to go! Unless you name a destination, you have no say in where you'll arrive.

Surely, life is not as simple as driving a car. Some things are out of our control. Many people have their world turned upside down by misfortune or a sudden tragedy. After a while they start to feel that their destiny is not theirs to determine.

Still, giving up on the right to guide your path in life is a dangerous state of mind. It guarantees that you won't come close to attaining your vision! On the day that you stop trying, you might as well be dead. We must seek to guide our destiny and create our future, regardless of past failures.

If the reader feels that such an attitude conflicts with their religious beliefs, it isn't meant to. While we may be blessed with talents and abilities, the responsibility to use them is ours. As French poet Jean de La Fontaine (1621–1695) said in one of his fables, *"Help yourself, and heaven will help you."*

In Picking Right, you should determine what you want. As covered earlier you must decide what's important to you, what you might compromise on, and what is absolutely unacceptable. Even if you don't believe that you could get your wish, you must still define it and go after it. Create your wish list, and use it as a yardstick by which to evaluate the opportunities that come your way.

Naturally, your requirements should be within reason as well as need. Can you find a millionaire who also looks like a model? Is that real or even necessary? If it is, then go for it. Otherwise, define what you need and want based on your goals for a relationship and for life.

A single parent needs a mate who is willing to raise kids that aren't his or her own. An artist should pick a mate who encourages his or her art and doesn't regard it as a waste of time. And a nine-to-fiver might have all of his or her values violated by a risk-taking entrepreneur.

The following real-life story illustrates what can happen when someone doesn't know what they want.

Sheryl was a single mother who hadn't formulated her wish list. About all she knew was that she hated being alone and wanted to be in a relationship.

She met a guy who lived on the opposite coast. They spent hours talking over the phone and laughing a lot. They "fell in love." She didn't know what she wanted anyway, so this looked promising. She up and moved with her child and dove into a relationship.

They were a mismatch, and the relationship was unhappy. But since Sheryl had no vision of her own to compare it to, she stayed in it for many years.

So it is vital that you define and know what you want.

YOUR RELATIONSHIP CHECKLIST

Years ago, before I met my husband, I decided to turn my mental wish list into a written checklist. I wanted to "know before I go."

I realized that the only way to have what I wanted in a relationship was to define it first. I had to decide what's important to me before I could find it. Whenever I met someone new, I could compare him to my checklist and know whether or not I was investing my time in the right person for me.

This sounds cold, you say. How about love and that spark that ignites between couples? How about "soul mates" and "chemistry"?

These are all very good, and I believe in love! But a man who dreams of spending his life on a farm shouldn't marry a city girl. And a woman who wants children had better fall in love with a man who wants the same. Love will not last in the face of serious discrepancies.

That's where your checklist comes in.

WHAT'S IMPORTANT

You have to ask yourself: *What's important to me in a relationship? What do I absolutely have to have in a mate? What do I refuse to have?*

Regardless of other people's opinions, only you can answer these questions. Some people may consider religious affiliation to be important. There may be ethnic preferences (but be sure they are *your* preferences too, not a family tradition that rules your life and ruins your happiness). Some artists find it important to share their life with another artist, others don't. These are all personal decisions that each individual must make for himself/herself.

BASIC NECESSITIES

That said, certain elements are vital and necessary. They should be placed at the top of your checklist, because when they are missing, there is no need to go further down the list.

(1) The person is single and available (not married and not in a relationship).

This is not a lesson in moral right and wrong. Getting involved with someone who is not available is impractical. It is a source of complications, if not worse.

Some people hope and wait for the unavailable partner to leave their mate and become "theirs."

Firstly, that doesn't always happen.

Secondly, if it does, you've just built your life over someone else's ruins; and if you believe in karma, that's not healthy.

Thirdly, you wouldn't want that done to you, so don't do it to another.

And lastly, you are bonding with someone who is obviously dishonest, because they had to cheat to be with you. If you are smart, you would predict the future based on their present behavior and go find someone who is available.

Almost anyone knows, and some have experienced, the many complications resulting from pursuing an unavailable mate. Don't do it.

(2) The person is emotionally available: he or she is ready for and desires a relationship.

Some people pursue partners who are stuck on their ex-mate. Or others who refuse to commit. Or someone who is so involved in their own personal turmoil, there is no room in their mind and heart for another person.

Investing yourself in such an individual is risky, and may not get you the happy relationship you long for.

This next real-life story is not uncommon.

When Mark and Brenda met, she informed him that she was still licking her wounds from her last relationship. She wanted to go out and have fun but was unwilling to get involved. During months of dating, Mark kept hoping for a change of heart, but it never came. Evidently he needed to move on and find someone who was ready for love.

Certainly miracles can occur, but why spend your life praying for a miracle when you can find someone who is as eager as you? After all, a person who is emotionally unavailable cannot give you what you want any more than a married person can.

Another type of unavailability is the guy or gal who wants to play around, date multiple partners, and who is unwilling to commit. My advice to you is simple: Move on! Don't waste yourself on a Player!

If you want a good mate, a friend for life, find someone who is looking for the same.

(3) The person is honest, dependable and trustworthy.

This needs no explanation. As covered earlier, it is a must-have.

(4) The person is drug-free and not an alcoholic.

The reader who is a drug user or an alcoholic may not like this aspect. However, what I say is the result of years of experience in the field of drug and alcohol treatment and prevention.

Drug users and alcoholics are a Wrong Pick. The worse the addiction, the worse the consequences. Drugs can take over a person's life. They have the power to destroy the user and ruin the lives of their loved ones.

In a relationship with a user, expect to be secondary in importance, the substance being his or her number one "love." And expect dishonesty and betrayal. They go hand in hand with addiction. From lying to theft, the addict will do anything to get their fix.

People sometimes latch on to addicts out of a desire to help. While that is admirable, it doesn't make for a happy relationship. You could make saving an addict your life's work and ruin yourself in the process.

If you can help it, don't start a relationship with an addict.

(5) Do not neglect the *Three Vital Rules*.

As covered in the chapter "Three Vital Rules for Picking Right," you want to make sure that the following conditions exist:

- You and your mate function at a similar speed.
- You have similar emotional attitudes toward life.
- Your goals do not clash but can be achieved side by side.

THE REST OF YOUR CHECKLIST

Now go ahead and extend your checklist until it contains everything you can think of that is important to you. It may include some of these qualities:

- The person is productive (hard working).
- The person is considerate, kind, unselfish.
- The person is affectionate, communicative, supportive.

Add anything else that is important to you. But focus on essential points. (Having a certain body type, liking similar food or music, may be nice but not essential to a long-lasting relationship.)

Remember, this is your life, and it's up to you to set your goals and find the person with whom you can achieve them.

USING YOUR CHECKLIST

How are you going to use your checklist? Obviously, you aren't going to run around town with a copy of it in your purse or pant pocket. You aren't going to inscribe it on the palm of your hand and glance at it when no one is watching. But you can keep it in mind when talking to people. Then between dates or conversations, you would refer to it and evaluate the situation.

GETTING ANSWERS TO YOUR QUESTIONS

How will you collect your information? How will you get answers to your questions? And how can you tell that you aren't being fooled?

There are two main methods, and you will need both.

(1) Observe

One method is observation. Observe the person's behavior, their interaction with you and others, what they say and what they do. Look and listen, as in this real-life example.

When Julie first met her future husband, she noticed that he was considerate toward his mother. They were close, yet Mom didn't run his life. In his business, he treated his employees decently. While he demanded productivity, he also rewarded hard work and granted second chances. These were all good signs.

Additionally, he didn't have great conflicts with the people in his life. He was ambitious and worked hard. And he was becoming a success in his own right, not by family connections.

You can find such things out by paying attention to what goes on around you, by observing actions and situations. Remember that truthful observation leaves no room for sugarcoating. You see what you see, and what you see is what you see. You will only go wrong if you overlook red flags or try to explain them away, as was the case in the following real-life example.

Lisa knew that Victor was disliked by most people. He was also quick to get into fistfights. "But he is sweet with me," she said, "and we have fun together. No one knows him like I do." Even when his violent disposition started to manifest in their relationship, she explained, "When he gets rough with me, it is because I nag and push him over the edge."

These were red flags, sugarcoated and nicely justified. But negative facts aren't less negative because we excuse them. Lisa failed to observe and be honest about her observations.

> *"A slender acquaintance with the world must convince every man that actions, not words, are the true criterion of the attachment of friends."*
> —George Washington

(2) Communicate

The second method of obtaining information is with direct communication. You need to talk to the person and ask questions.

For instance, don't wait for someone to tell you whether or not they are in a relationship. *Ask!* Of course, a Player might lie to you, but the truth will come out sooner or later. If they lied, throw the relationship into the trash bin without regret. This person isn't worth it.

Young people in particular often wonder, "How do I find out?" You ask! "But isn't that too direct?"

There is a mistaken notion in our society that direct communication is rude. It is not. In fact, we need more of it.

I much prefer it when a man asks me early in a conversation if I am married. Some men beat around the bush with indirect questions while glancing at the ring finger. I spare them the agony by mentioning my husband. Now it's out in the open, and I need not worry that my friendliness might be misconstrued.

When dealing with a prospective mate, you need to know where you stand, and as soon as possible. Communication is your best tool.

THE INTERVIEW

During a job interview, questions are asked of the interviewee in order to determine whether or not he or she could fill a position. In a relationship "interview," you question your "prospect" in order to determine whether or not you are potentially a match.

This may sound cold and calculated, but this is your life and happiness we are talking about and, for that matter, theirs. The decision cannot be made lightly.

Would you purchase a house without first researching the area for safety, quality of schools and other factors? Would you put down money (your love and life) on a house without proof that it has clear title and is available for purchase (the person is unmarried and available)? A relationship may lead to greater decisions than buying a house and should be regarded accordingly.

As in any interview, you ask questions. Your checklist guides your line of questioning. I have personally employed this method, and having been happily married for several decades I can attest that it works.

When I first met my husband I asked if he was married or in a relationship. Once I found out that he was available, I asked about previous relationships, and wanted to know how they went and why and how they ended. A person may not tell all, but you get an idea, and also get a sense of what they might not be saying.

Then I asked about his occupation. "A rich man" was not on my checklist, but "a competent man" was. Money can come and go, but talent, skill, intelligence and a strong personality aren't lost. A competent and dynamic mate has what it takes to survive life's storms and build a future together. Our abilities are the only security we have. They are the only guarantee that, should we fall, we can rise again. So I wanted to get to know him and know that he, not his pocketbook, was amazing.

I also wanted to know about his relationship with his family. Bitterness and hostility may be signs of heavy mental baggage. Additionally, I looked into any signs of drug or alcohol use. I left no stone unturned.

My husband still jokes that I gave him the "third degree." I even questioned the fact that he was younger than I, until I realized that his maturity more than made up for it.

Naturally, the *interview* is not an interrogation. You don't sit the person down and question them to death. You communicate back and forth and find things out over time. Perhaps you were satisfied with what you initially found out and start dating. While dating, keep asking questions and finding out more. Then don't forget to compare what you find out with your standards and requirements as outlined in your checklist. That's important, as you will see here.

Rick and Donna were a couple in their thirties who got along marvelously, except for one issue: Donna wanted kids—the sooner the better. She had traveled the world, had gotten an education and had a successful career. She felt that she had no time to waste.

In Rick's mind, he was just getting started: His career was taking off, he was growing his investments, and he had aspirations to travel the world. While he was true to Donna, he didn't want the limitations and obligations that come with having a family, for at least another decade.

If Rick and Donna compared their relationship to their respective checklists, they would see the discrepancies. Being a mismatch, yet loving each other, makes for a tough decision. As hard as this may be, if you don't determine your own path, life carries you where it will. Wouldn't *you* rather call the shots?

So create your checklist and refer back to it again and again. Observe well. Ask questions. Conduct your "interview."

And make no mistake: while you interview him/her, he or she is *interviewing* you!

SOME INTERVIEW QUESTIONS

- Are you married? (If the answer is yes, end the interview.)

- Are you in a relationship? (If yes, end the interview.)

- Have you been married before? What happened? What is the current situation?

- Prior relationships? What happened? What is the current situation?

- Any children? Where are they? Who is the other parent? What is the current situation?

- Employment/business? How do you make your livelihood? How is it going?

- What are your plans/goals in your professional life?

- What are you looking for in a relationship?

- What are your plans/goals for a relationship?

- Do you want children? How many? When?

- Are you Christian/Jewish/Muslim, etc. (whatever is important to you)? How religious?

- What is your opinion/attitude toward drugs and alcohol? Any drug/alcohol use?

As you talk to people, you will come up with additional questions. Grant yourself permission to ask them, and your conversations will be fruitful and enlightening. Soon enough you will know whether or not you are a good match. If so, you stay. Otherwise, continue your search until you find the Right Pick.

RELATIONSHIP CHECKLIST SUMMARY

If you want to Pick Right, do the following:

- Decide what *you* want.

- Create your Relationship Checklist.

- Conduct "interviews."

- Compare what you find out to your checklist.

- Draw conclusions and make your decisions.

Having and using a checklist takes the guesswork out of Picking Right and puts you a step closer to having the happy relationship you have always wanted.

So don't be shy. Ask your questions. Your happiness depends on it.

EXERCISE 13
Your Relationship Checklist

Note: It is recommended that you use a separate sheet of paper or
make a copy of the next page. Your checklist may change or grow as you
meet people and discover more precisely what you need and want.

Creating your *Relationship Checklist* may wind up being a turning
point in your life. If previously you have traveled the relationship
jungle not knowing your destination or what you are after, from
this point on you will have guidelines and set standards against
which to measure all relationship opportunities, challenges and
possible pitfalls.

Below is your basic *Relationship Checklist*. It is up to you to
add to it anything else that is important to you. In the future, you
may decide to include additional points or delete things you now
consider unimportant. Keep in mind that you are molding your
own future. Be true to yourself and shape your vision the way you
have it within you.

But remember this: Whatever qualities you expect of your
Right Pick, be sure to have these yourself. Otherwise, not only
will it be unfair, but the discrepancy could be detrimental to the
relationship.

YOUR CHECKLIST

- ❏ Single and available (not married or in a relationship)
- ❏ Emotionally available
- ❏ Honest, dependable, trustworthy
- ❏ Drug-free and not an alcoholic
- ❏ Comparable "speed" to yours (Vital Rule #1)
- ❏ Comparable "emotional approach" to yours (Vital Rule #2)
- ❏ Your goals do not clash but are attainable side by side (Vital Rule #3)
- ❏ Productive
- ❏ Considerate, kind, not selfish
- ❏ Affectionate
- ❏ Communicative
- ❏ Supportive

- ❏ _____
- ❏ _____
- ❏ _____
- ❏ _____
- ❏ _____
- ❏ _____
- ❏ _____
- ❏ _____
- ❏ _____
- ❏ _____

CHAPTER 14

*I*NGREDIENTS OF LOVE THAT LASTS

CHAPTER 14

*I*NGREDIENTS OF LOVE THAT LASTS

While this book is about Picking Right, it would be irresponsible of me to leave you without a word of advice to help you the rest of the way.

Providing you have Picked Right, what can you do to build your relationship into a strong, stable union *and* preserve it? What should you avoid that could destroy it?

This chapter supplies a partial list of vital ingredients for a successful relationship and some tips to help you on your journey.

RESPECT

A happy relationship must include mutual *respect.* What does that mean to a couple? The dictionary defines *respect* as "high regard for or a sense of the worth or excellence of a person." This means that they think highly of one another, and each feels that the other is a wonderful and excellent person.

Suppose one of them wanted to go back to school. They wanted to advance their career, earn more money and have greater satisfaction in their work. If their mate had *high regard* for them, had *a sense of their worth or excellence*, he or she would support them all the way. He or she would believe in them and feel that they were capable of making their dreams come true. That is *respect.*

Suppose your mate wanted to lose weight—*a lot* of weight. If you respected them, you would cheer them on and try to help. You wouldn't constantly remind them how they gained back all the weight they had lost on the last diet. You would be there for them and admire them for trying again. That is *respect*.

Some couples struggle with this: One or both try to restrain the other's development because of their own insecurities. They are afraid that if their mate became more successful or better educated, he or she would outgrow them.

In such cases, it is up to the person who aspires to grow to make their mate feel safe and secure. And it is up to the insecure mate to recognize the negative effect they are creating and to restrain their urge to keep their partner down. It takes a lot of good communication between the couple, until cooperation is achieved.

But a relationship cannot be successful without the partners having and displaying mutual respect.

ADMIRATION

How do you feel about a performer or an artist whom you admire? You marvel at their works and abilities. You have faith in them. You think of them with awe. They are *awe*some to you. Even if they struggle in life or suffer some bad press, you cheer them on and wish them the best. You think they are fantastic!

That is how you and your ideal mate should regard each other. Admiration is a combination of respect and strong affection. It is a vital ingredient that makes the difference between a happy relationship and a dull one, between success and failure. Yet it is often missing.

In place of admiration we commonly see this: He says, "I need to protect her and care for her," because he doesn't think she is sufficiently strong or able. She says, "He always makes mistakes, and I don't believe in him." Perhaps she even feels sorry for him and has an urge to help him.

Wishing to help is honorable, but it isn't a healthy ingredient for a lasting relationship. As noted earlier, you don't want sympathy; you want *admiration*.

The word *sympathy* comes from Greek *syn*, meaning "together" and *pathos*, meaning "suffering." Many couples "suffer" together. They commiserate with one another.

A much better way to help someone you love is to admire them. Believe in them, and then send them out into the world to win some battles.

Consider this: What are your mate's positive attributes? What does he or she do well? What talents does he or she have? Anything— from cooking to repairing a leaky faucet; from being kind to being ambitious, hardworking or helpful. Find something positive about him/her, and *love* it!

Chances are they will become more successful, thanks to you, to your positive attitude and the trust you put in them. Because behind every great person there is a great mate, and a relationship filled with mutual admiration has the highest potential of lasting a lifetime.

FRIENDSHIP

You and your match should be friends. *Good* friends! The dictionary tells us that *friendship* involves *affection as well as a willingness to help.* Your friends like you and are willing to be there for you in time of need. They support you in your endeavors and want to see you succeed. They advocate for you: should someone speak against you, they will protest it. Additionally, you can confide in them without judgment or disapproval and trust them to never use your secrets against you.

A relationship should include friendship. A couple should be there for each other: to overcome challenges; to help make individual as well as mutual dreams come true; to lend an ear, encourage, brainstorm; to plan and do, win or lose. They should be willing to talk about everything and go through good and bad times together, like friends would.

HONESTY AND TRUST

As covered earlier, without honesty and trust, a relationship is doomed to fail. Couples who *are* happy together are happy because they can trust each other. When trust goes out the window, so does happiness.

Trust means that you can rely on your mate to not violate your agreements. You know that nothing is going on behind your back, and that he or she has nothing to hide except for, perhaps, the surprise birthday party they are planning for you or that special Christmas present you've been asking for. Needless to say, you yourself must be equally trustworthy.

There is a personal policy I live by in my marriage of nearly three decades: I never do anything I wouldn't want to tell my husband about. If I'd have to hide it, it must be wrong. So I don't do it. It's that easy.

Not only is mutual trust vital, but it takes the stress out of life and makes it so simple!

> *"Human happiness and moral duty*
> *are inseparably connected."*
> —George Washington

CRITICISM / FAULTFINDING

Critical people tend to find fault in anything and anyone. They don't look for virtues; they find flaws. They would rather point out your mistakes and tell you what is wrong with you than compliment your positive qualities or good actions. Some call such people "negative."

Children, teenagers in particular, are seen to criticize their parents. We hear parents criticize their children for "getting bad grades" or "not helping around the house." Such criticism seldom helps. Have you ever known a child who improved by being told how *bad* they were? Have you ever benefited from having your flaws and mistakes pointed out to you?

Although critical people would justify their criticism as well meant or "constructive," we must ask ourselves whether "constructive criticism" even exists. Just recall how you felt last time you were "constructively criticized." Did it make you a better person? Did it motivate you or boost your confidence? I doubt it.

It is interesting to note that we get what we stress. If we stress the negative, such as mistakes, bad behavior or failure, we get more of that. Remind someone of all the times he or she was late, and you will get more tardiness. Tell the guests how badly a child behaves, and you will get more bad behavior. Sit there contemplating your past failures, and you'll become convinced that you can do nothing but fail.

The opposite is also true. Focus on the positive—success, good intention, constructive action—and you will get more of that. You can even go as far as *disregarding* the negative altogether, not even *mention* another's mistake. Instead, highlight the positive, compliment them on *anything* they do right, and they will start to do more right than wrong. It is an interesting experiment. Give it a try.

Extremely critical people look for and stress the negative, the wrong, the mistakes and the failures. Ask yourself: *How critical is your mate of you? How critical is your mate of his or her boss, parents, friends, or even ex? Does he or she focus on how wrong everyone else is or how inadequate?*

You possibly believe that some criticism is justified. Perhaps you are often tardy, and someone criticizes you for being late. In that case, you say, the critic is right. Certainly there is nothing wrong with asking you to be on time, but that is not criticism. A critic makes you *wrong* for being late, points out that you are "always" late, and throws your other flaws in the mix. You may have noticed that some people make a "big deal" out of your mistakes while others are more forgiving. So, some are more critical than others. Why?

People criticize because they feel badly about their own misdeeds. Perhaps *they* used to be habitually late. Now they are critical of anyone who is late. Or perhaps they took a dollar bill out of somebody's wallet and did other things they weren't proud of. Now they hope to feel better by catching others in the act. In other words, criticism is a sign of a guilty conscience.

This is so true that if your relationship started off well but now your partner is critical of you, it's a sure sign that they are doing something they shouldn't be doing or are not telling you something they feel you should know. Similarly, if you become critical of them, you must soul-search for what you have done to them that you keep secret.

Secrets are the curse of a relationship. They build a wall between the partners and make them grow apart. Even if those secrets are small, the effect is the same: the wall grows taller, partners become critical of each other, and the mutual admiration they once had is replaced by faultfinding. A relationship goes downhill from there and will fall to ruin.

A good partner is someone who is not overly critical. If they suddenly *become* critical, get them to read this chapter as well as chapter 11, "Are You Ready for Your Match?" and have them do Exercise 11, "Your Self-Confession." If they change and can keep their nose clean from then on, the potential for success is high—that is, if you act the same.

> *"Any fool can criticize,*
> *condemn and complain—*
> *and most fools do."*
> —Benjamin Franklin

CARING AND SUPPORTIVE

It has been said that life is no picnic. To be truthful, it is more like a battleground. Even daily life can be overwhelming: from financial stress, work and career hurdles to family matters and health issues. We need help. And we must recognize that others need *our* help.

If life is a battleground, we better make our relationship the base where tired and wounded soldiers may recuperate before returning to the front line.

When someone has been challenged all day, had to prove themselves to the boss, nearly lost a deal, argued with mother over the phone, got bad news from the doctor or has just been pushing themselves for days without proper food or sleep, they hope to find a safe haven in their mate. They need their support.

Being supportive requires that we observe the condition our mate is in when they return from battle and help them recuperate from their misadventures. It means lending an ear, *without* pointing out that they are wrong, even if they are. Before they recognize that the boss, mother or whoever was right after all, they might need to vent the disappointments of the day. Then, when the realization is theirs, not something that was pushed off on them, they may benefit from it. Otherwise, they'll reject any words of wisdom.

Being supportive also means urging them to keep going. If a business deal fell through or they failed a college exam, they don't need anyone's sympathy or encouragement to quit. Doing so is like telling a wounded soldier to give up and stay in the wheelchair for life. Do give them care; let them rest; then send them back on their way with your faith and support to win their next battle.

You want a caring and supportive mate, and in turn you must be caring and supportive of them.

TOLERANCE

Every person is unique and no two people are the same. Siblings, even twins, do not have identical personalities. Evidently there is a spiritual quality to people, separate from their physical makeup, which makes them who they are. Some call it "spirit" or "soul"; some talk about "energy" or "life force." Whatever the name, this quality cannot be measured by blood tests and has nothing to do with brain chemistry. It is nonmaterial, but it exists.

Have you ever known two people who were raised in the same environment, had similar upbringings, yet followed different paths in life? Perhaps their neighborhood was crime ridden, but one turned to crime while the other became a successful professional.

In other words, individuals are unique. Or, in the words of a three-year-old who made this observation about his family, "We are all special and different." Indeed!

Because each person is unique, we must permit people to *be* who they are without disapproval or criticism (providing it isn't harmful,

164

of course). Have you ever met a parent who couldn't accept their child as he or she was? They had aspirations *for* the child, only they didn't bother to ask what the child wanted for himself or herself.

I am reminded of a pianist who suffered his parents' disapproval because, they said, "Music is not a profession." The absurd part of it was, their criticism continued even after he had become one of the top performing pianists in his field! They were so busy being disappointed in him for not becoming who they wanted him to be that they couldn't acknowledge his accomplishments. They simply refused to accept who and what he was.

As noted, one's "uniqueness" must not be harmful to others. You are not going to say, "He likes to torture kittens, but that's just a part of his personality, so we should accept the way he is." In a relationship, a woman wouldn't carry the financial burden alone because "he needs time to find himself." A man should not do what one man did: provide all financial support while his wife "traveled the world" on her own, doing nothing in return. Similarly, one would not permit sexual promiscuity because "that's just the way he or she is."

In other words, you draw the line where "uniqueness" becomes destructive. Do not tolerate it if it is harmful or makes you miserable in the relationship.

However, providing your mate is not mean, lazy, promiscuous, or anything else that you can't live with, they should be appreciated as the person that they are. There should be no complaining, nagging or faultfinding about their nature or character. Don't try to change them into someone they are not. It isn't fair. If they don't fit your ideals, and you really don't like the way they are, don't have a relationship with them.

Similarly, your unique personality should be accepted, admired and respected despite the differences between you.

Men and women *are* different from each other. A guy might like to restore old vehicles, while his girl sees no joy in getting dirty out in the sun and going back and forth to the auto store for parts.

In the same way, a woman can drive a man crazy talking about hair, makeup, or solutions for PMS. We have seen the agonized faces of men who follow their ladies around a department store while they shop.

Even though our differences may present challenges, they are also an asset. We complete one another. Together, a man and a woman may have more good qualities that make a better life than each has on his or her own.

If a couple can tolerate each other's unique personalities, they may have the best of both worlds. If they *admire* one another, they may find exceptional happiness together.

Men and women should let each other *be*, regard their differences with tolerance, and love and respect one another for *who* and *how* they are.

Life would be better all around if we lived by this old poem:

> *There is so much good in the worst of us,*
> *And so much bad in the best of us,*
> *That it hardly behooves any of us*
> *To talk about the rest of us.*
> —Anonymous

THE ART OF PRESERVING GOOD INGREDIENTS

While your relationship may have all the right ingredients, your success depends on your ability to protect and preserve them.

You wouldn't take a carton of fresh milk and leave it out in the sun. Similarly, you mustn't abuse a good relationship by violating your agreements, mutual trust and respect, or by neglecting to continuously nurture your union.

Many couples are mainly guilty of failing to preserve and nurture what they have started. Once they've been together for a while, they stop working to keep romance going, to take pleasure in each other, or to maintain good communication between them. They put the relationship "on automatic" and expect it to keep going with little effort of their own. As mentioned earlier, they neglect the "garden" that is their union. Uncared-for gardens wither and grow weeds that threaten to destroy them.

Preserving the ingredients of a good relationship takes work. You must remain alert to any deterioration of your communication or affection toward each other. Good communication is the powerful weapon with which to cure any conflict or disagreement you might have. Use it to heal your upsets, to establish and reestablish your agreements.

Try to be patient and kind toward each other. Try to be friends to one another. Consider yourselves comrades in battle, and keep the battle on the outside, not between you. Make home the refuge where you each find safety, reassurance and support. Your relationship is an oasis in the desert, where you regain your strength and get ready to once again meet the world.

That's what a worthwhile relationship should be like. So don't settle for less. Pick Right, and then preserve all the good you've created. As long as you keep up your "gardening," there is no reason why your union shouldn't blossom forever.

Picking Right: The Single's Guide to Finding the Right Match

EXERCISE 14

Creating and Preserving Vital Ingredients

If you are in a relationship, or when you start one, do the following:

1. Have your mate read chapter 14.

2. Discuss each ingredient with him/her and try to reach agreement on each point.

3. Reach agreement as well on the section titled "The Art of Preserving Good Ingredients."

4. Together, do all you can to follow these guidelines and keep your "ingredients" fresh.

A VALUABLE TIP

You will find that when one or both of you are tired, hungry, ill, under the influence (even as mild as a glass of wine), or it's "that time of the month" for her, you are "not yourselves."

Such circumstances make a bad time for discussing relationship issues. A matter that may be resolved calmly could turn into a heated quarrel when you aren't at your best physically. Therefore, food, sleep, getting sober, and whatever else may be required to bring you and/or your mate back to normal must come first.

Make it a rule to discuss your differences *only* when you are both well fed, well rested, drug-free and sober.

168

A POINT SYSTEM

When working with couples, I use a point system. Such a system helps determine how well the relationship is going: is it improving or worsening?

This is much like measuring business success by keeping track of its income. Unless you know how much money the business earns and can compare it week to week or month to month, you don't know whether it's on the rise or the decline.

In business and relationships alike, a point system provides an objective means by which to measure progress. Relationships, more than business, are subject to emotions, causing us to lose objectivity. External influences such as work challenges or illness can cause stress that impacts the relationship. It is helpful to differentiate between such stress and what is happening between the couple. A suitable point system provides a way to measure how well the relationship is going regardless of what else may be happening in life.

EXAMPLE

A good day together	+ 10 points
A particularly happy day together	+ 20 points
A minor upset	− 5 points
A major upset	− 10 points
Not speaking to each other on day(s) following an upset	− 10 points

You may use the above point system or create your own. Whatever your system, it should reflect how well you are doing in creating and preserving the *Ingredients of Lasting Love.*

CHAPTER 15

*R*ECIPES FOR HAPPINESS

CHAPTER 15

RECIPES FOR HAPPINESS

 People want to be happy. Young or old, rich or poor, more educated or less, we all seek happiness. When we can't find it on our own, we look to someone else to make us happy. But the truth is, it is up to us to generate our happiness, and on the day that we stop creating it, we won't have any.

Some couples become dependent on each other for their individual happiness. This works to a degree, particularly at the beginning of a relationship. But if it continues, and if one or both are unable to be happy in his or her own right, the relationship becomes strained.

> *"Peace comes from within.*
> *Do not seek it without."*
> —Buddha

IS IT POSSIBLE TO GENERATE HAPPINESS?

Some people believe in fate, luck or destiny. Leaving your future in the hands of the Fates, with no guidance of your own, is a dangerous gamble. This book is for people who seek to *guide* their destiny. Life dishes out enough unpredictability, disappointments and even tragedy. Whatever faces us, let's not take it lying down. We must strive to generate our own happiness and live our dreams; or else, why live?

Whether in a relationship or not, and regardless of what goes on in your relationship if you have one, there is always *something* you can do to improve your situation. There are always *some* factors you *can* control that will make things a bit better.

For instance, you can always set a goal, no matter how small it may be, and work to attain it. You will find that if you work toward your goals and make progress on the path to their attainment, you will start feeling better. You will in fact be generating some happiness.

> *"Diligence is the*
> *mother of good luck."*
> —Benjamin Franklin

GOALS AND YOUR HAPPINESS

Goals are essential to happiness. People who have no goals are unhappy. It's as simple as that.

Have you ever known an aimless teenager? Are they trying to accomplish anything? No. Are they happy? No. Do you see the correlation? A person who isn't pursuing some goal will be unhappy.

Some parents soul-search endlessly in an effort to discover where they went wrong: What might they have done to make their child unhappy? Usually, it isn't what they *have* done but what they haven't. Unless they've helped the child set goals and work to attain them, he or she will be purposeless and unhappy.

Most youths turn to drugs because they are bored. They lack goals, either because they already have everything or because they feel hopeless about being able to achieve anything. Drugs offer some excitement to counteract the agony of boredom. They generate new problems and provide new "goals" to achieve: avoiding getting caught; lying without being found out; stealing to support their habit. These are goals, destructive as they may be. And they provide something to do, challenges to overcome and a "game" to play.

People need a game. Without goals to attain, there is no game, no life and, also, no happiness.

Consider old folks: The goal of raising a family has been attained, and the kids have moved out. They are no longer needed like they used to be. They retire. They don't have to do much. They pass the time, pleasantly or unpleasantly. They get busy aging.

What goals do they still have? How to avoid slipping in the shower and breaking a hip? How to have their diapers changed without losing too much dignity? Without new goals, the aging process accelerates. They get dementia. With the help of modern medicine, they can live for years as a vegetable using up their long-term-insurance benefits. But they aren't happy.

It is interesting to note that dementia (defined as "a general term for a decline in mental ability severe enough to interfere with daily life") commonly occurs after retirement age. Is that a coincidence? Or could it be this has more to do with running out of goals than with physical deterioration?

I am reminded of an artist friend of mine living in Europe who, in her nineties, still sculpts, holds art shows and does community service. She pursues her goals and is happy and relatively healthy. I believe she is destined for a long life and to being sharp as a tack to the day she dies.

> *"When you're finished changing,*
> *you're finished."*
> —Benjamin Franklin

A RECIPE FOR HAPPINESS

There is a recipe for happiness, and you can use it to create your life much like a chef creates a banquet. It will enable you to uplift yourself if you are down and to generate your own happiness.

Consequently you'll be a better mate and a better spouse. You'll be an asset to your relationship and have a positive and constructive influence on the person with whom you share your life.

But be forewarned: This recipe is simplicity itself. If you expect some complicated instructions, you may be disappointed.

TRUTH IS SIMPLE

Many years ago, a friend gave me an invaluable piece of advice (I was having a bad day). "Whenever I am down," he said, "I go help someone. It always makes me feel better." I never forgot this nugget of wisdom and have used it beneficially time and time again. It never fails to work, because it is true. Yet it is simple.

> *"The best way to cheer yourself*
> *is to try to cheer somebody else up."*
> —Mark Twain

Truth *is* simple. If you think back to some helpful advice you've received from a parent, teacher, mentor or some other significant figure in your life, it was simple, wasn't it? Most of the time we respond to truth with, "Well, of course! I've known that!" We recognize it when we see it.

Deep inside, you know the truth: about yourself, relationships and life; except that you haven't been acknowledged for knowing and have sometimes been made wrong for it. You've been told that your elders know best, that truth is complicated, and that it can only be found in thick, hard-to-understand books written by authors who have multiple initials after their names. Yet all along, truth has been inside of you, simple and easy to grasp.

Complicated "solutions" can't be true, because if they were, they would be simple—and they would work.

Have you ever met someone who, after years of therapy or other work, "understood" what was wrong with them, only it was still wrong with them? Obviously they haven't found the truth, or they wouldn't still be trapped by the very issues they now "understand."

"Truth will set you free." Truth leads to solutions. When such solutions are put into effect, they bring about change and improvement.

With truth, you can do something about life to make it better for yourself and others.

And truth is simple.

The following *Recipes for Happiness* are simple. The first one deals with you. We start there, because you must be happy as yourself before you can be happy as someone's mate.

> *"Sometimes the*
> *questions are complicated and*
> *the answers are simple."*
> —Dr. Seuss

EXERCISE 15
Creating Your Individual Happiness

To be happy you must continuously have goals and work to attain them. Your basic *Recipe for Happiness* is as follows:

1. Set a goal (any goal).

2. Work to achieve it.

3. Make good progress, and then (do not skip the next step)...

4. Once you have achieved your goal, set a new one and work to achieve it.

Then repeat these steps over and over.

Achieving a goal or reaching a mountaintop is not the key to happiness. It is the fruitful *journey* that makes for happiness, not the arrival. Once you've arrived, you may rest on your laurels for a day or a week; but then look ahead and choose the next "mountain" to climb. Otherwise, your happiness will fade away.

In the words of Benjamin Franklin, "There will be sleeping enough in the grave." Until then, keep setting goals and working to achieve them. "Can't I ever relax?" you ask. Of course you can. But even if you desire a vacation, you are still striving to achieve a goal.

> *"Roads were made for
> journeys not destinations."*
> —Confucius

EXERCISE 16
Creating Your Happiness as a Couple

In spite of its simplicity, the recipe laid out below gets violated by most couples, as illustrated in this real-life story.

When Steve and Kathy met, their first goal was to get to know each other. They did so, and they were in love. Next they went on a long trip to Europe, spending every moment together, and survived that. So far, so good.

The new goal was to get married, which they did. Buying a house was next, and that was accomplished. Both were settled into jobs, so their employment goals had been attained. Children were born, and all seemed to be well.

It was at that point that they failed to set new goals. What did they want from and for each other? How could they help one another? What should they do together? They had already reached the peaks of the "mountains" they had aimed for: travel, jobs, a house, kids. What was going to be their next summit? Without new goals, their interest in each other began to wane and their relationship started losing its luster.

To preserve your happiness as a couple, use the following recipe:

1. Employing good communication, agree on a goal or goals. These may be relationship goals or your individual goals, which you will help each other to achieve.

2. Work together to achieve your goals.

3. Make good progress.

4. Once a goal has been attained, set a new one.

Repeat steps 2, 3 and 4.

EXPANDING YOUR HORIZONS

Once your basic relationship goals have been achieved, what else could you strive for? A lot. For instance, if you remember that the world needs help—a lot of help—you'll never run out of "mountains" to climb. The people of the world are our brothers and sisters, so to speak. They are our extended family. How could we regard ourselves as true winners if the world we live in is losing?

There is always something out there, a group or a cause, that should be helped. A couple could become comrades, not only in raising their own family, but in helping others.

Nothing compares to helping people. If we help successfully, we might become the happiest people on Earth. So help each other; help your families; help your community and the world.

> *"The best way to find yourself*
> *is to lose yourself*
> *in the service of others."*
> —Mahatma Gandhi

BONUS CHAPTERS
WHAT'S IN THEM FOR YOU?

The following three chapters were written after *Picking Right* had been on the market for over two years. During that time feedback from readers poured in, both verbally and in writing.

While some reported life-changing realizations that had broken them loose from the suffering of past relationships and in several cases led to happy marriages, others remained stagnant despite the insight they had raved about after reading the book.

This bothered me greatly. I love results. I *live* for results! I want positive transformation for every one of my readers who is in search of solutions.

An analysis of many cases ensued, and my conclusions led me to write this additional material. It reinforces a number of the principles covered earlier in the book, which each of my "failed cases" had neglected to accept and use. Since those principles can make or break your life, I devoted to them chapters 16 and 17. Chapter 18 answers a few questions not covered in the first edition that readers kept bringing up.

One more point is yet to be made, which will determine whether you gain positive transformation from this book or none at all. The following real-life story illustrates it best.

Rebecca was a beautiful single woman in her thirties—the kind of beauty who turns heads when she walks into a room. She was highly educated, intelligent and ambitious. She could not find her match, and the men she dated did not rush into commitment.

*Two years after I had first met Rebecca I asked if she had found her match. Since still she hadn't, I recommended that she read my book. Not because it is **my** book but because I know for a fact that **failing to achieve something is a sure sign that one does not know all there is to know about it.** Think of the cook who keeps burning the food. He or she obviously has more to learn about cooking.*

Rebecca's explanation of her failure to find a match was that "American men were not good enough" for her. If nothing changes in the next two years, she said, she would go back to her home country, where she would have no problem finding a husband.

If, like Rebecca, you think you know everything, you will learn nothing! Your *attitude* makes the difference between changing your life with this text and simply adding it to the long list of relationship books you have read with no results. Realize that if you have not found your match or if you keep Picking Wrong, you need *new* tools to help you Pick Right.

While reading this book, did you do the exercises? They were created for *use*, not for show. Because I know how painful it can be to tackle the subject of relationships, I carefully designed the exercises to take you on your journey in baby steps, from light to heavy.

How about the glossary at the end of this book? It contains not merely definitions but nuggets of wisdom to bring the reader a new and unique view on life and relationships. You will find *love, courtship, happiness, marriage* and more defined in a whole new way that offers new understandings. With better understanding, you *can* succeed.

Naturally, every person is different and some circumstances are extremely challenging. If after doing everything I recommend in this edition you are still "stuck," contact me for coaching.

I hope these bonus chapters will increase the reader's chances of getting positive results from this book, for that is my mission!

"Being ignorant is not so much a shame as being unwilling to learn."
—Benjamin Franklin

CHAPTER 16

CUTTING LOOSE

CHAPTER 16

CUTTING LOOSE

Why is it that so many singles can't find their match?

In my experience, the biggest reason is that they are stuck in the past, in earlier relationships. They are still mourning the loss of a former mate or being bitter from the hurt of a previous relationship. In other words, they never turned the page.

When a person is licking their wounds, their "vision" is impaired: the right person could be standing directly in front of them, and they wouldn't see him or her. That's because they are not "present" in the here and now.

You cannot build a desirable future from the past. You have to come into the present first, because the future can only be created from "now," never from "yesterday."

When Ruth came out of an abusive marriage, she mourned her past. Not the loss of her husband—that, to her, was "good riddance." But she grieved her youth—the years she had wasted with an unworthy man, who didn't value her beauty, devotion or kindness.

Because she saw the world through the mist of her past, she couldn't see the men she met for who they really were. Every man resembled her "evil ex-husband," and she refused to commit.

And so she remained single until the day she died.

Being stuck in the past can ruin your life. Can you imagine trying to build a successful business when everything reminds you of your past failures?

> **"To be wronged is nothing,**
> **unless you continue to remember it."**
> —Confucius

Many old people are stuck in the past, and they constantly think and talk about their past. Our "retirement mentality" is largely at fault for that. It sends the message that a retired individual can no longer create a future. They have done their share, and they can now rest. Rest, until they "rest in peace"! And so retirement can be more of a curse than a blessing.

My client was a school teacher who loved her work and the children whose lives she touched. Eventually she reached "retirement age" and was forced to retire. Twelve years later she was so sickly she could hardly function.

Retirement may be fine for someone who despises their job and can't wait to be free of it. But forcing into retirement someone who loves their work and who is making a difference is a sure way to destroy the person.

If you are struggling to find your match, ask yourself: Do I still have attention on someone in my past? Who is he or she? What should I do to unstick my attention from this person and put the past behind me?

If you are still struggling, unable to cut loose from the past, reread chapter 10, "How to Make a Fresh Start," and chapter 11, "Are You Ready for Your Match?" and do the exercise at the end of each chapter. Even if you have done these exercises before, do them again, this time keeping in mind all the information in this book.

The following letter from one of my readers (who read the first edition of this book) might inspire you:

"I did the exercises in your book — each one in sequence. At the end I had ended all attention on past relationships. About a week later I met her.... That was amazing! I didn't even know that I had much attention at all there. Well, thank you for that." —Robert B

If you still get nowhere, contact me for coaching by filling out the contact form on my website www.TheSecretsOfHappilyEverAfter.

You CAN move on and find happiness!

> *"Never regret yesterday.*
> *Life is in you today and*
> *you make your tomorrow."*

— L. Ron Hubbard

CHAPTER 17

WHAT YOU MUST KNOW ABOUT HUMAN NATURE

CHAPTER 17

What you must know about human nature

In chapter 14, "Ingredients of Love That Lasts," I touch on criticism or faultfinding—those people who are quick to point out others' mistakes. There is more I wish to share with you on this subject, as understanding it can change your life; maybe even save it.

We've all been taught that people are mad at us because of what we did to them. We have wronged them somehow. We said something mean or destroyed something that was dear to them, and now they are bitter and talk badly about us.

It is true that being cruel or rude to people, scratching their cars for fun or stealing their finest clothes isn't the way to make friends. If you go around making enemies, you *will* accumulate them. So, naturally, you should treat others the way you want to be treated.

But how about those times when you have tried your best: you haven't stolen anything from this person, you haven't deceived them, you haven't been mean and you tried to be helpful. Yet this person is critical of you. They tell you (and maybe everyone else) how bad you are. They pick fights and blame you for being this way and that, for disrespecting or mistreating them (when you haven't tried to). Nothing you do resolves the situation. They might even claim you have been so mean that they must terminate their relationship with you and can no longer be your friend, lover, spouse or employee. They have got to leave!

If you know you haven't tried to do the things they accuse you of, then the reason they hate you is not what you have done to them but...what they have done to you that you don't know about.

"Oh," you say, "this couldn't be." Think again. Investigate, and you may find what this critical person is hiding from you.

Jerry and Suzanne had been married for several years. When Jerry announced that he was leaving the marriage, he out of the blue came up with a list of never-before-heard complaints: his wife didn't make him feel like a real man and didn't treat him like a man. He wasn't happy, and she was the reason why.

This was sharp but general criticism. He couldn't even come up with specific complaints, since she worked, cooked, cleaned and took care of him as a wife. She was affectionate and they had good communication and a normal sex life.

The truth was he had to justify the fact that he was having an affair with another woman, and the only way he could excuse this was to find fault with her, whether real or imagined.

Have you ever experienced, witnessed or heard of similar circumstances? That's criticism.

When we fail to uncover the person's wrongdoing, we feel puzzled and confused (which Suzanne did). But realize that unjustified faultfinding is a sure sign of guilt. It means unkind actions have taken place against you without your knowledge. There is no exception to this rule!

Of course, you shouldn't believe me. Instead, start looking around you and see for yourself whether or not this is true.

If your girlfriend is eyeing your boyfriend, she will become critical of you. She will start making disapproving comments or judgments. It could be about anything: how self-centered you are; how you never think of her; nobody likes you; you never do for her as much as she has done for you; and more. People get quite imaginative when they have something to hide!

So if someone dislikes you for no reason, know that he or she has done something to you that you don't know about—such as the coworker who hit on your girlfriend at the party and is now talking behind your back or trying to get you fired.

This is human nature, and if you understand it, you can save yourself a lot of grief.

A critical person is a red flag, in any type of relationship. If you meet someone new and they are critical of their friends, coworkers, family—you name it—know that you haven't met a poor victim. On the contrary, they are doing things to the people they are bad-mouthing that those people don't know about.

This is the reason that, should you meet a married or attached person, you should never ever believe the horror stories they tell you about the wife's or husband's mistreatment of them. Realize that their talking to you behind their spouse's back is only one of the dark secrets they keep from him or her. And having secrets, they become critical.

Now, you may not like what I have to say next: If you find that you are being critical of another (out loud or quietly, to yourself), ask yourself, "What have I done to this person that he or she doesn't know about?" If you truly can't think of anything, it may be that you have *failed* to do something that you should have done or were counted on to do. Perhaps the wife didn't pay a bill on time and now, to make herself feel better, she shines the spotlight on her husband's errors.

So, yes, this chapter also gives you a way to keep your own conscience clean and your heart happy. And that's a bonus!

Again, this is human nature, and a valuable aspect of it to understand and use.

EXERCISE 17

Understanding Human Nature

1. Can you think of someone you have not harmed who dislikes you, has been critical of you or has wanted to end their friendship or relationship with you? Write down his or her name.

_____

2. Do you know what he or she has done to harm you or what they may be hiding from you? If so, note it down briefly.

_____

_____

Repeat the above with three other examples.

1. _____

2. _____

_____

1. _____

2. _____

_____

1. _____

2. _____

_____

CHAPTER 18

*W*HERE TO MEET PEOPLE

WHERE TO MEET PEOPLE

My client was a twenty-eight-year-old professional: beautiful, intelligent, single and looking. Although she wasn't new in town, her biggest challenge — she thought—was *where* to meet single men.

Where is the wrong question, because people are everywhere: the grocery store, the bank, the library, the coffee shop, the post office, business networking, community groups, clubs, parties, and the list goes on. Unless you live on a desert island, there are people everywhere you go!

What puts the power to meet new people in *your* hands is having the right *attitude*: You could either wait for someone to approach you or for another to introduce you to that person—or you could simply reach out and make it happen yourself. The former makes you passive. The latter makes you proactive.

"But how?" you ask.

You walk into a coffee bar and stand in line to order your drink. In urban America, many people avoid eye contact, refrain from smiling and are terrified of saying hello, as if they are going to catch something. When I first arrived in the US, straight to Los Angeles, I couldn't believe people could be so withdrawn. It was a culture shock. True, you may find yourself engaged in some strange conversations

(I have!), but they won't go on forever and won't kill you. On the other hand, who knows what good might come of it?

Our modern-day culture is a lonely place, where people fear communication. Their phone is a safe "friend." When they look it in the eye, it doesn't look back. It doesn't ask personal questions. They can safely talk to people who aren't present. Whatever happened to communicating with someone who is right there?

I walked into a grocery store one day and saw a lady wearing a shirt with a bright sunflower design. I smiled and said how I felt: "Your shirt brightens up this place!" She replied, "And you brighten it up with your smile!"

The world is starved for communication. With it, we can uplift each other. Sometimes in an instant. You can put a smile on someone's face at no cost to you, by commenting on a nice outfit, a good hairstyle, a unique piece of jewelry, their child or their dog.

I was at a stoplight on my bicycle one day when a man crossed the street wearing red shoes. "I like your shoes," I exclaimed; "my favorite color too!" He lit up.

Clearly, he had put some thought into picking those shoes, and that someone had noticed them cheered him up. It didn't endanger my life, it was no embarrassment, nor did it cost me a dime. And I was paid back with a friendly response!

> **"Let us always meet each other**
> **with a smile, for the smile**
> **is the beginning of love."**
> —Mother Teresa

But let's get back to you standing in line waiting for your coffee. You could smile and say hello to the person next to you, whether of the same or opposite sex. You could talk about the weather. You could even ask a personal question such as, "Do you work nearby?"

I am not talking about "hitting on" people, but simply reaching out and being friendly. If nothing else, you'll lighten the atmosphere and loosen up some uptight people. In the future, you may run into the same person again. Strangers could become acquaintances. Acquaintances may become friends. You'll expand your social circle, and with that you'll meet more people and increase your chances of finding your match.

So it's not that you don't know *where* to meet people. It's what you do with the people you meet. And what you should do, regardless of whether or not you are interested in a relationship with someone, is make friends!

Naturally not every friend is a potential "match." Perhaps you get acquainted with someone just to find out that he or she is married or is in a committed relationship. Fine! You have gained a new acquaintance. A man might go home to his wife and say, "I've met this nice lady at the coffee shop. I think we should introduce her to my brother Bill."

My point is, don't wait for things to happen. *Make* them happen.

> *"Every path but your own is the path of fate.*
> *Keep on your own track, then."*
> —Henry David Thoreau

BEWARE

A comment I have heard repeatedly from my readers and from those attending my talks on the subject is that the principles of "Picking Right" are as relevant to business and interpersonal relationships as they are to romantic life. Indeed, they are!

Now that you are making new friends, this is a good time to use your knowledge of "red flags" with everyone, not only romantic interests.

Have you ever made a "friend," only to be stabbed in the back by him or her? Looking earlier, weren't there warning signs that you had ignored until it was too late?

Fortunately, today is a new day: for the first time, you are holding in your hands the manual for Picking Right, the guide to choosing your people in *any* type of relationship. So use it well!

WHAT TO DO

Reread chapter 6, "Telltale Signs," and chapter 7, "Types of People." Next, do the exercise at the end of chapter 7, using it with every new person you meet and get to know.

If you have a romantic interest in a new person, be sure to ascertain whether he or she is truly available: single and not in a relationship. Because this person isn't connected to anyone else in your life, you don't have "reliable sources" to verify his or her relationship status. So use your "red flags" knowledge well.

There is one more thing you must keep in mind: birds of a feather do flock together. The company your new friend keeps gives a clue as to who he or she is. Do his friends get drunk or have extramarital affairs? Do her girlfriends hang out in bars and leave with a new guy every night? Anyone who condones such behavior in their friends probably acts the same.

Vickie was a stripper. She met her boyfriend in the strip club where she worked. Once the relationship got "serious," she quit her job and they moved in together. It turned out he was unfaithful and a pervert. She was heartbroken, and they split up. But isn't that what you would expect of a man who hangs out in strip clubs?

* * *

James met his future wife in a bar. As the years rolled by, her drinking took its toll on the relationship. He despised the way she acted when she was drunk, and she got drunk a lot.... That's what people do in bars: they drink and get drunk. So if you meet him or her in a bar, don't be surprised if his or her drinking is heavier than you suspect.

Depending on what you are looking for, put yourself in the type of environment that your ideal match frequents. It may be networking meetings, hiking clubs, college, church, libraries or charitable organizations.

Again, if you use the "smile and say hello" method of getting in friendly communication with people, you'll grow your social circle and develop a larger pool for Picking Right.

> *"Don't compromise yourself.*
> *You are all you've got."*
> — Janis Joplin

SHOULD WOMEN "HIT ON" GUYS?

The following story was told to me by a frustrated single guy:

Tony used to work for a company where he was friends with a lady coworker. Several years after leaving the job, he ran into her and found out that she had gotten married and had a child. She confessed that, while they worked together, she liked him but didn't say anything. His reaction was, "Why didn't you tell me?!"

He'd had no idea! At the time she used to share "boyfriend stories" with him, which made him think that she had no interest in him. They were "just friends." In hindsight, he wished he had known.

"Women should hit on guys," Tony said to me. "Guys also want to be courted and pursued. If she had only said something…"

I think Tony has a point!

Nowadays, so many people aren't open. They pretend. They play games. They are afraid to be outgoing. Romantic comedies lead the way in teaching both men and women how to be fake and insincere in their approach to one another. While this may be funny on screen, it will get you nowhere in your love life.

Nothing replaces being boldly open and honest. Both men and women should let their intentions be known. What are you afraid of? Rejection isn't fatal. On the other hand, "hinting" and hoping you are understood could wind you up like the girl in the above story, who probably wonders what her life would have been like had she given her coworker a chance.

"Happiness is when what you think,
what you say,
and what you do are in harmony."
—Gandhi

EXERCISE 18
Where to Meet New People

Make a list of places you go where you meet people:

_____   _____

_____   _____

_____   _____

_____   _____

Make a list of additional places you could go to meet more people:

_____   _____

_____   _____

_____   _____

_____   _____

_____

Make a list of activities you could get into where you would interact with people:

_____   _____

_____   _____

_____   _____

_____   _____

_____   _____

IN CLOSING
The Missing Ingredient

The pages of this book are filled with basic principles, methods and tools to help the reader Pick Right. However, one ingredient is missing here, an ingredient only you can provide: the ability and, indeed, the *courage* to make a decision.

The word *decision* comes from a Latin word meaning "cutting off." When one makes a decision to break up, he or she is *cutting off* from their relationship partner. When two people decide to tie the knot, they are cutting off from a single life and any potentialities it may have.

If a couple chooses to have children, they commit for life, and their decision is irreversible, since they can't "send the kids back" to whence they came. If they decide to remain childless, they might regret it down the road when it's too late.

As hard as this may be, life requires that we make decisions. When we stand we aren't sitting. When we sit we aren't walking. We can't do both actions simultaneously, nor can we live multiple lives at the same time.

But decisions are not only something we *must* make; they are choices we need to make for our own sake. The worst state to be in is that of indecision. A "maybe" guarantees nothing but unhappiness.

Have you ever been in a relationship with someone who wouldn't give you a yes or a no? Your life was one big maybe. You weren't sure that you were wise to stay, but you also weren't certain that you should go. Without clear-cut decisions, nothing happens. Maybes prevent progress and action. If potential buyers can't decide to purchase a house, the house remains unsold. Action requires decision.

An inability to decide usually stems from fear of making a mistake. Some people date endlessly and never tie the knot because they are afraid to discover that they've made the wrong decision. At the same time, they don't break up for fear that doing that would be a mistake. They live in a maybe.

If at the close of this book you still suffer from indecision or have maybes in your life, go back and review earlier chapters. Take the time to do the exercises again. Read the glossary at the end of the book. And *apply* the information to the trouble spots in your relationship.

To be happy and successful we must make decisions, not go with the flow. Any decision is better than no decision, because it eliminates the maybes that drive us crazy and allows progress and action.

Then the outcome, be it good or bad, is the result of our own determination, not someone else's doing. Later we can look back on our life and say, "I did it my way."

> *"I've lived a life that's full,*
> *I traveled each and every highway;*
> *And more, much more than this,*
> *I did it my way."*
> —Paul Anka

BUILD LIFELONG RELATIONSHIPS
THAT STAND THE TEST OF TIME
FREE Relationship Course Shows You How

Sign up now for your FREE course
and make lasting relationships a reality.

Go to www.TheSecretsOfHappilyEverAfter.com

RELATIONSHIP COACHING
In Person or over the Internet

Get help to
- Pick Right
- Keep It Right
- Salvage It When It Goes Wrong

Go to www.TheSecretsOfHappilyEverAfter.com
or CALL 626-888-7759

"I will help you find your Happily Ever After!"
—Daphna Levy

ABOUT THE GLOSSARY

This glossary contains valuable information and expanded definitions as they relate to relationships. Be sure to make use of it to deepen your understanding of these key concepts and help you to Pick Right.

GLOSSARY

admiration: When we *admire* someone we have a feeling of liking and respect for them; we feel great affection for them while, at the same time, holding them in high regard; we think that they are wonderful. This word comes from Latin, meaning "to wonder" and "wonderful." *Admiration* is lacking in just about all relationships. Most couples are either obsessed with each other or grow critical of one another. If such attitudes were to be replaced by mutual admiration, the relationship would elevate to a whole new level of pleasure, stability and love. It would become a great source of empowerment for both partners.

attraction: *Attraction* is the feeling of liking someone and being drawn to them sexually. Some people have a "lasso effect" on those of the opposite sex: they get ahold of you and you feel pulled in to them like a piece of metal to a magnet. While such obsession may be exciting, it is rarely a guarantee of a Right Pick. More often, it is a sign of future trouble, because the obsessive attraction prevents you from thinking straight, detecting red flags and making the right choice.

commiserate: When we *commiserate* with someone, we show them pity or sympathy for their sorrow or trouble. It's a pretty useless activity, since it doesn't assist the person in pulling out of their misery. On the other hand, they will not respond well to "cheering up" either. Fortunately, *something* can always be done to help them: Make sure they eat nutritious food and get some sleep. Have them get any needed medical care by a competent physician, because they might have a medical condition that contributes to their unhappiness. Get them off drugs or alcohol (with proper drug/alcohol treatment or medical supervision). Sometimes taking them out for a walk can do wonders (see Exercise #8, "Gaining Clarity"). Just don't sit there helping them drown their sorrow in a bottle; you'll both wake up the next day with a hangover. That's a pretty poor form of "help."

courtship: *Courtship* is a lost art. Some dictionaries even refer to it as old-fashioned. It's the activities and time spent by two people who are pursuing each other for the purpose of marriage or romantic involvement. Nowadays this step is often omitted, which gets many people into relationships they wouldn't otherwise choose to have. They are much like an employment seeker walking into a business and starting to work without knowing what kind of a person the boss is, what their pay is going to be or how employees are treated.

criteria: Your *criteria* are the principles, standards or factors that you use to make your decisions. *Criteria* is plural for *criterion.* Many people haven't established their criteria for a relationship partner or a relationship. They don't know what they are looking for. That is their first problem. You are not going to arrive at your destination if you haven't decided where you want to go. Some people would discourage you from establishing your own criteria. They would tell you that you can't get what you want in life, that it's all fate, so why bother? Such a fatalistic view—all is predetermined and you are powerless to change it—is dangerous. It is the road to misery. Even religious people recognize that God helps those who help themselves. The word *criteria* comes from Greek, meaning "to separate or decide." With good relationship criteria you can separate the good from the bad and make the right decisions for you. See chapter 13, "Your Relationship Checklist," and the exercise that follows.

demonstrative: A *demonstrative* person exhibits or expresses his or her own emotions, especially those of love or affection. Most young children are demonstrative. Some women are more demonstrative than men, although this is not always the case. Some couples experience difficulty because one of them is more demonstrative than the other. In truth, this needn't be an issue. The demonstrative mate should keep the character differences in mind, and the less-demonstrative one should accept their partner's displays of affection. This goes back to mutual tolerance, as covered in chapter 14, "Ingredients of Love That Lasts," under "Tolerance."

emotion: *Emotions* are feelings that range from joy to boredom, anger, hatred, fear, anxiety and sorrow, down to complete hopelessness and despair. We think of our emotions as being separate from our thoughts, but our emotional reactions should not justify illogical behavior. (It did Romeo and Juliet no good to act on their emotions and not a drop of logic.) Emotions can get in your way: You know that you should confront someone with the truth, but you are *afraid*; you know that you should apologize, but you feel *angry*; or you know that you should move on, but you can't face the *sorrow* of breaking up. Emotions are overrated. Just as the road to hell is paved with good intentions, so it is paved with misplaced emotions that could prevent you from making the right choices.

genetic: *Genes* are the part of the cell that determines physical characteristics. *Genetic* characteristics are physical traits, such as facial features, body build, complexion, hair and eye color, which are passed on through the genes. The word *gene* comes from Latin, meaning "born, produced; race, kind, kin or relative." So genetic similarities have to do with the body, and they transfer from generation to generation. On the other hand, intellect, talent and ability are not inherited by physical means, if at all. Every person is unique. A child might learn from his parents or wish to imitate them, but such similarities are not *genetic*. Conditions such as addiction, depression and insanity are not genetic either, and contrary to popular belief, no evidence or conclusive tests exist to show that they are.

gullible: Someone who is *gullible* is easily tricked or deceived. This usually happens because they refuse to see the red flags that are waving in their face. They are afraid of trouble and wish to avoid problems and tough decisions; so they convince themselves that there is no trouble and ignore all signs of it. Consequently they wind up with disaster. Trouble doesn't go away just because you say it isn't there. To Pick Right and have happy relationships, you must keep your eyes wide open and see what's in front of you. *Gullible* comes from a word meaning "to swallow." Indeed, a gullible person "swallows" the lies and deception fed to them by unworthy people, for which they pay the price.

happiness: The sense of joy or contentment that we call *happiness* is a condition that is best created by the person himself/herself. Some unhappy people get into a relationship hoping it will bring them happiness. This could become a great burden on their mates. You should have goals and dreams that you pursue and personal accomplishments that make you joyous and proud. Then you will have positive emotions to bring into a relationship. If both partners are content, each in his or her own right, together they will experience even greater happiness. However, if they are miserable in their individual worlds, they will bring negativity to the relationship and will be a drain on each other. Soon they will believe that the relationship made them unhappy. Not so: they brought their unhappiness into the relationship and being together did not remedy it. But remedying individual unhappiness is not the role of a relationship. A relationship isn't there to "save" you; its role is to enrich and empower you further. Except that *you* must provide a good foundation on which to create even greater happiness.

harmony: In music, when different tones join to create a combination that is pleasing to the ear, we have *harmony*. In relationships, when two people join and create a union that brings them happiness, that is *harmony*. Harmony is agreement, and it depends on the partners having similar views and feelings about things. The more agreement they have, the more harmonious the relationship. The more disagreement, the more inharmonious it will be. A couple might create so much disharmony that they can no longer coexist. The word *harmony* comes from a Latin word meaning "to join together." Harmony is synonymous with unity, peace and friendship. If you want harmony, stress your agreements, your similar views and what you have in common and disregard the petty differences.

hypocritical: A *hypocritical* person pretends to have feelings, beliefs, principles or qualities they don't actually have. The word comes from Greek, meaning "play the part." Indeed, a hypocritical person plays whatever part they feel will get them what they want. They are not to be trusted nor are they to be respected, because this person is a coward. They haven't the courage to be who they are and to present themselves to the world the way they really are. Obviously, they have no self-respect if they think they must alter themselves to be accepted or to make their way in the world. Hypocritical people are a liability in anyone's life and are a Wrong Pick in relationships.

love: *Love* is a strong feeling of affection toward someone. Some people confuse love with attraction (see *attraction* in this glossary). Being attracted to someone could mislead you into believing that you love them. The "lasso effect" that is attraction is the source of the confusion. Real love for a sexual partner is not unlike the love you have for a child, a parent or a good friend. The main difference is your intimacy. And so *love*, that deep affection and bond between you, can last into old age, even through illness and other circumstances that may inhibit sexual activity.

marriage: *Marriage* is a partnership, a union, a bond. It is more than a legal arrangement. It is more than a commitment. There is more to this union than a familial and economic bond. For a marriage to be successful, it must have uninhibited communication between the partners, or their union starts to deteriorate. Communication can remain free only in the absence of deception and harmful lies. So honesty and trustworthiness are a part of the definition of *marriage*. The purpose of marriage is to *assist and enhance the lives of all concerned*. That tells you what a bad marriage is: it fails to do so or, worse yet, it produces the opposite effect.

myth: A *myth* is a false idea that many people believe to be true. The word comes from Greek *mythos*, meaning "a legend or story." There are many myths regarding relationships. No wonder problems are as common as they are! If truth will set you free, then it follows that *un*truth will trap you. Myths hide solutions to problems. They prevent understanding. Without understanding something, you can't do anything about it. So when it comes to relationships, it is vital to separate the myth from the truth. One clue to the presence of myths is the inability to find solutions: If you find yourself stuck in a problem that won't resolve, know that you are dealing with *myths* and don't relax until you find truth.

probation: *Probation* is a period of testing or trial of someone's conduct or character. At the start of a relationship, both of you are on probation; you are testing and observing one another to determine whether or not you are compatible. Probation is necessary. The word comes from Latin, meaning "to test and find good," which is exactly what you do with a new person in your life. Give it some time, observe carefully, and make sure the person passes probation.

relationship: A romantic relationship follows all the basic principles of marriage. The main difference between a *relationship* and a marriage is the level of commitment: Most unmarried couples have not committed themselves to each other for life yet, or they have not made their commitment official in the eyes of the church or the law.

Like a marriage, a relationship should be beneficial to all concerned. Its purpose is to *assist and improve the life, health, happiness and success of its members.* A relationship must be truthful. Any hypocrisy or dishonesty undermines the communication between the partners and so weakens the relationship. It is such communication breakdown that usually brings it to an end.

respect: A person who feels *respect* toward someone has *high regard for or a sense of the worth or excellence of that person.* A happy relationship must include mutual respect, which means the partners think highly of each other. Most people will treat you the way you treat them. If you are respectful, admiring, loving, it is only a matter of time before others start treating you in kind.

responsibility: Some people think of *responsibility* as being accountable, being at fault or having to justify one's wrongdoing. Responsibility has become synonymous with blame, making it something we all wish to avoid. A more empowering approach to responsibility describes it as "being the author or cause" of a condition or situation. And so, without considering yourself "at fault," you can still see your part in bringing it about. This is a helpful approach, because it says that you aren't a helpless victim of your fate but can do something to guide it and, hopefully, build a better life for yourself and those you love.

sympathy: *Sympathy* and commiseration are very much alike. When you feel sympathy for someone, you feel sorry for them. The Greek roots of the word mean "to suffer with." Indeed, you "suffer" with this person. In relationships, some people choose mates they feel sympathy for. That is a recipe for disaster. The relationship can be expected to be emotional and filled with drama. It is going to drain the sympathy-giving mate. At the same time, the sympathy-absorbing person will require more and more sympathy, which proves he or she was not helped by it. Pick someone you respect and admire, not someone for whom you feel sorry.

HELPFUL RESOURCES

As drug and alcohol abuse have the power to destroy the best of relationships, I am providing here some resources to help readers in their search for solutions and drug-free alternatives.

The responsibility for the use of this information is entirely yours.

Safe Harbor—*International Guide to the World of Alternative Mental Health* provides non-drug approaches for treating mental health issues.
www.AlternativeMentalHealth.com

Peter Breggin, MD—author of several books about prescription drug addiction, including *Psychiatric Drug Withdrawal: A Guide for Prescribers, Therapists, Patients and their Families.*
www.breggin.com

The Road Back—a free eBook: *How to Get off Psychoactive Drugs Safely.*
www.theRoadBack.org

Drug and Alcohol Rehabilitation
Narconon—a worldwide network of drug and alcohol treatment centers that do not use drug substitution.
www.NewLifeRetreat.org
877-905-5772

Editing and Proofreading
Rosemary Delderfield
E-mail: rdeld@hotmail.com
Tel/Fax: 727-461-6163

Art Direction and Design
Eugenia May-Montt
www.maymonttgraphics.com
E-mail: emaymontt@gmail.com

Typography and Graphic Production
Lea Frechette
E-mail: lea.goartists@gmail.com

ABOUT THE AUTHOR

Daphna Levy-Hernandez was born and raised in Israel where she completed her schooling and served in the Teachers' Corps of the Israeli armed forces. Early in life she traveled the world, visiting many countries, living and studying on three continents.

The urge to make a difference motivated her from an early age. At fourteen years old she volunteered to tutor underprivileged children and kept at it until her graduation from high school. Years later she and her husband founded a nonprofit organization dedicated to drug-abuse prevention among youth.

In the eighties, long before *life coaches* were popular, Daphna fulfilled her calling with the launch of a rewarding consulting career. *Relationships* soon became her area of expertise, as she found they often interfere with able people's happiness and success. She has helped hundreds with individual coaching and touched the lives of many others in her seminars and workshops.

CPSIA information can be obtained
at www.ICGtesting.com
Printed in the USA
BVOW03s2039070917
494291BV00001B/33/P